THESSALONIKI TRAVEL GUIDE

2024-2025

Navigate Like A Local: Uncover The Top Attractions And Iconic Destinations.

CHRISTY R. INGRAM

Disclaimer

The information contained in this travel guide is for general informational purposes only. While every effort has been made to ensure the accuracy of the information provided, prices mentioned in this guide are approximate and may vary. Addresses, business hours, and other details may change over time, and travelers are encouraged to confirm these details directly with local establishments before making any plans or bookings.

The author and publisher make no representations or warranties of any kind, express or implied, about the completeness, accuracy, reliability, suitability, or availability with respect to the information provided. Therefore, any reliance you place on such information is strictly at your own risk.

The author and publisher disclaim any liability in connection with the use of this information. Readers should exercise their own due diligence and verify details such as prices, addresses, and services before traveling.

CONTENT

INTRODUCTION

Nestled in the heart of Northern Greece, Thessaloniki is a bright reminder of the country's rich past and lively contemporary culture. It is Greece's second-largest city, combining ancient grandeur with contemporary attractiveness, making it an irresistible tourist destination. Thessaloniki, with its lively streets, rich cultural tapestry, and spectacular views, captivates visitors from the moment they arrive.

Cassander of Macedon founded Thessaloniki in 315 BC and named it after his wife. It has played an important role in numerous historical periods. It has served as a crossroads of civilizations and cultures, from its status as a significant city of the Byzantine Empire to its time under Ottoman administration. Each layer of history has left its mark, transforming Thessaloniki into a living museum where ancient ruins interact with modern life.

Located strategically on the Thermaic Gulf, the city boasts a magnificent shoreline that offers breathtaking views and a bustling environment. Thessaloniki is a city where the past and present blend harmoniously, providing visitors with a variety of experiences ranging from visiting Roman ruins to enjoying fashionable cafes and boutiques.

The city's importance and appeal

Thessaloniki's attractiveness stems from both its historical significance and its dynamic current culture. It is a city where ancient traditions seamlessly merge with contemporary tendencies. This mix provides a setting that is both innovative and familiar, making it a desirable destination for a diverse spectrum of visitors.

The city's historical significance is vast. Thessaloniki, a significant port city, has long been a crossroads of cultures and people. The architecture, cuisine, and traditions reflect Roman, Byzantine, and Ottoman influences. The Rotunda, a large circular building that was originally built as a mausoleum for Emperor Galerius and later converted into a Christian church and mosque, encapsulates the city's rich history. The White Tower, another renowned emblem of

Thessaloniki offers panoramic views of the city and a glimpse into its medieval past.

However, Thessaloniki is more than just a relic of the past; it is a bustling modern metropolis. The city's active nightlife, rich food scene, and cultural festivals make it an exciting trip. The lively Aristotelous Square, dotted with cafes and shops, is the center of the city's social life, bringing inhabitants and visitors together against the backdrop of exquisite neoclassical architecture. The city's markets, including Modiano and Kapani, are vibrant with the colors and aromas of local produce, spices, and traditional cuisines.

One of the city's greatest strengths is its ability to serve everyone. History buffs can explore the city's numerous ancient sites and museums, including the Museum of Byzantine Culture, which holds an impressive collection of Byzantine antiquities. Meanwhile, visitors looking for relaxation and recreation can visit the city's many parks, seaside promenades, and beaches. The city's culinary culture is equally diversified, ranging from traditional Greek tavernas serving classic meals such as moussaka and souvlaki to modern restaurants serving inventive Mediterranean cuisine.

Thessaloniki is particularly known for its festivals and cultural events, which contribute to the overall exhilaration of any visit. The city hosts a number of festivals throughout the year, including the Thessaloniki International Film Festival, which draws filmmakers and cinephiles from all over the world, and the annual Dimitria Festival, which celebrates music, theater, and dance and features both local and international talent.

For those looking to venture outside the city limits, Thessaloniki is a wonderful entrance to Northern Greece. The surrounding Halkidiki peninsula, with its gorgeous beaches and crystal-clear waters, is only a short drive away and provides an ideal hideaway for anyone wishing to unwind in nature. Furthermore, the scenic villages and historical places in the surrounding area offer several chances for day trips and exploration.

What genuinely distinguishes Thessaloniki is its friendly and welcoming environment. The city is recognized for its welcoming residents, who are always willing to share their culture and traditions with visitors. Whether you're meandering through the tiny streets of Ano Poli (the Old Town), savoring local foods at a bustling market, or sipping a sunset cocktail at a seaside tavern, Thessaloniki will welcome you with open arms.

Thessaloniki is a city that smoothly integrates its rich historical history with a vibrant and modern lifestyle. Its unique position as a civilizational crossroads has given it a rich and dynamic personality that attracts all types of visitors. From its ancient ruins to its modern cultural scene,

Thessaloniki provides a varied experience that is sure to captivate and inspire. Whether you are a history buff, a foodie, an explorer, or simply someone wishing to experience Greece's beauty and charm, Thessaloniki is a location that will not disappoint.

Embrace Thessaloniki's charm, where every nook tells a tale and every encounter contributes to the city's rich mosaic.

CHAPTER ONE

Preparing for Your Trip

Traveling to Thessaloniki, Greece's bustling northern gem, is like opening a treasure chest full of delights. Before you enter into the rich fabric of this city, a little forethought can transform your trip from a simple vacation to an amazing journey. Here's your definitive guide to preparing for a fantastic trip to Thessaloniki, along with all the crucial tips and techniques to help you make the most of your visit.

Planning & Research

Dreaming of Thessaloniki.

The first step in planning your trip is to let your imagination travel around the lively streets of Thessaloniki. Begin by researching the city's highlights and distinctive offerings. Explore internet travel forums, blogs, and this guidebook to learn about must-see destinations, local traditions, and hidden gems. Websites such as TripAdvisor and Lonely Planet provide useful traveler reviews and recommendations.

Creating your itinerary

Once you've gotten a feel for what Thessaloniki has to offer, plan your agenda. Consider your hobbies, whether they are in historical locations, gastronomic trips, or outdoor activities. A well-planned itinerary strikes a mix between sightseeing and downtime, giving you time to enjoy the city's vibrant culture.

Sample Itinerary

Day One: Arrival and Exploration

Morning: Arrive in Thessaloniki and settle into your accommodations.

Afternoon: Walk around Aristotelous Square and the seaside promenade.

Evening: Have dinner at a typical taverna and sample local cuisine.

Day Two: Historical Immersion.

Morning: Visit the Rotunda and Galerius Arch.

Afternoon: Visit the Museum of Byzantine Culture.

Evening: Relax at a café in the Ladadika neighborhood.

Day Three: Cultural and Culinary Delights

Morning: Explore the local marketplaces, including Modiano and Kapani.

Afternoon: Participate in a culinary class or food tour.

Evening: Enjoy Thessaloniki's nightlife at a trendy bar or live music venue.

Day Four: Day Trip and Outdoor Fun.

Morning: Visit the surrounding Halkidiki peninsula or Vergina hamlet.

Afternoon: Relax at the beach or go on a nature hike.

Evening: Head back to Thessaloniki for a quiet meal.

Local Etiquette

Understanding local customs and etiquette will enhance your trip and allow you to easily fit in with the Thessaloniki mood.

Greetings & Interactions: The Greeks are famed for their warmth and kindness. A pleasant handshake is customary, and it is appropriate to greet people with "Kaliméra" (good morning) or "Kalispera" (good evening). When entering a store or restaurant, a nod or grin is always welcomed. Check the glossary page for more phrases.

Dining Etiquette: In Thessaloniki, dining is more than just eating; it's a social event. When dining out, it is usual to share meals, so don't be afraid to try a little of everything on the table. Tipping is not required, but a small amount (around 5-10%) is appreciated if you receive excellent service.

Dress Code: Thessaloniki is somewhat casual, yet modesty is recommended, especially while visiting churches or religious places. You'll most likely be touring the city on foot, so bring some comfortable walking shoes.

Traditions and customs are highly valued in Thessaloniki due to the city's long history. When visiting religious or historical places, show respect and adhere to any restrictions or rules that may be in place.

Packing Essentials

Packing intelligently guarantees a smooth vacation, allowing you to fully enjoy Thessaloniki.

Clothing

Comfortable Shoes: The streets of Thessaloniki are frequently cobblestoned, so sturdy walking shoes are required. A pair of comfortable sandals or sneakers will do you well.

Weather-appropriate attire: The weather in Thessaloniki varies. Summers are hot and dry, so bring lightweight, breathable clothing and a wide-brimmed hat. Winters are milder but can be wet, so pack a light jacket and layers.

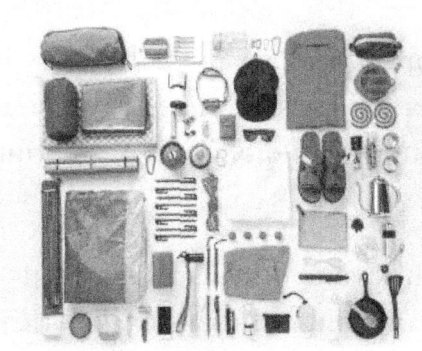

If you plan to visit churches or monasteries, bring modest clothes that cover your shoulders and knees. Women may wish to carry a scarf to cover their heads if necessary.

Other essentials

Sunglasses and sunscreen: Wear shades and use high-SPF sunscreen.

Reusable Water Bottle: Stay hydrated while exploring. Thessaloniki is warm, so keeping a water bottle accessible can keep you hydrated.

Adapter and charger: Greece uses a conventional European plug with two round prongs. Bring the appropriate adaptor for your equipment, and don't forget your chargers.

Travel Guides and Maps: While cellphones are useful, having this printed guidebook or map can be invaluable, especially if you're venturing off the main road.

Travel Documents

Having your travel documents in order is critical for a successful vacation.

Passport and Visa: Make sure your passport is valid for at least six months after your planned stay. Determine whether you need a visa to enter Greece based on your nationality. Most EU citizens and many others can enter Greece without a visa for short stays.

Travel Insurance: Purchase comprehensive travel insurance that covers medical emergencies, trip cancellations, and lost possessions. It's a tiny fee to pay for your piece of mind.

Keep records of your accommodation and transportation reservations. Digital versions on your phone and physical copies in your travel folder may be beneficial.

Health and Safety Tips

Staying well and safe is essential for enjoying your Thessaloniki vacation.

Health precautions

vaccines: Determine whether any vaccines are required for travel to Greece. Hepatitis A and B immunizations are common, although particular requirements may differ depending on your health and travel history.

Local Healthcare: Thessaloniki has excellent medical facilities, but make sure your travel insurance covers medical expenses. Carry a modest first-aid kit with essentials such as bandages, painkillers, and any personal medications.

Cuisine and Water Safety: Thessaloniki's cuisine is typically safe to consume. However, as with any new location, stick to well-cooked dishes and bottled or filtered water to avoid gastrointestinal problems. Local street cuisine is typically wonderful, but choose vendors who maintain rigorous cleanliness standards.

Safety Tips

Personal Safety: Although Thessaloniki is a relatively safe city, normal measures should be taken. Keep a watch on your belongings, particularly in crowded areas. To secure valuables, use a crossbody bag or money belt.

Familiarize yourself with the local emergency numbers. In Greece, the emergency numbers for police, fire, and ambulances are 112.

Be aware of the local laws and regulations. For example, it is prohibited to consume alcohol in public places other than licensed institutions. Following local rules will help you have a smooth and pleasurable journey.

By meticulously planning, you set the stage for an unforgettable vacation in Thessaloniki. You're ready to experience the wonders of this enchanting city now that you've planned your itinerary, packed your belongings, and have all of the necessary documentation. From the moment you get off the plane until the final farewell, Thessaloniki promises a journey rich in history, culture, and amazing encounters. So pack your luggage, grab your camera, and prepare to discover one of Greece's most enchanting places!

CHAPTER TWO
Journey to Thessaloniki

Traveling to Thessaloniki is like entering a fairytale, with each chapter containing exciting experiences waiting to be discovered. This chapter will help you navigate every step of your journey to Greece's second-largest city, from the minute you leave home until you arrive. Let us break down the steps to ensure that your journey begins as smoothly as a perfectly prepared Greek coffee.

Getting to the Airport

Your trip begins the moment you leave your home, so make a well-organized strategy for getting to the airport. Whether you're coming from a local city or flying in from another continent, here's how to make this leg of your journey as smooth as possible.

Domestic and International Flights

Domestic flights

If you are going from within Greece, getting to Thessaloniki is simple. The city is well connected to major Greek towns such as Athens, Heraklion, and Rhodes. Greek domestic airlines, including Aegean Airlines and Olympic Air, fly often to Thessaloniki. These flights are often short and comfortable, with the journey from Athens to Thessaloniki taking approximately 50 minutes.

International flights

Are you traveling from overseas? Macedonia Airport (SKG) in Thessaloniki is an important transportation hub. The airport is well connected to several European cities and beyond. Major airlines, including Lufthansa, British Airways, and Turkish Airlines, provide direct flights to Thessaloniki. Depending on your departure city, you may be able to discover cheap airlines that offer competitive tickets.

Transportation Options for the Airport

By car:

Driving to the airport provides flexibility and convenience. If you're leaving your car at the airport, make sure there are long-term parking choices accessible. Most airports offer both short- and long-term parking options. To get the best rates, try to book in advance.

By Taxi

Taxis are a convenient way to get to the airport. They provide door-to-door service, which might be especially useful if you have a lot of luggage. In many places, you can reserve a taxi in advance or find one at designated taxi stands. Always clarify the fare with the driver before beginning your journey to avoid surprises.

By Public Transportation

Public transportation is often a cheaper choice. Many cities have specialized airport buses or trains that link key districts to the airport. To ensure a pleasant ride, check your local timetables and routes ahead of time. If you're traveling during busy hours, try departing a little early to allow for potential delays.

Air travel

Booking Tips

Book early to get the best rates. Prices typically grow as the departure date approaches, particularly during high travel seasons.

Compare airfares: Use flight comparison services such as Skyscanner or Google Flights to compare airfares from various airlines. This might help you locate the most cost-effective solutions.

Flexible Dates: If your travel dates are flexible, use fare comparison tools to look into other options. It is sometimes possible to save money by flying during the week or at off-peak hours.

Check luggage policies: Ensure that you understand the luggage policies of the airline you are flying with. Budget airlines frequently have tougher baggage policies and costs.

Sign Up for Alerts: Many flight booking services provide price alerts. Sign up to receive updates when the price of your flight changes, allowing you to get a fantastic deal.

What to expect at the airport.

Before you fly:

Check-In: Most airlines provide online check-in, allowing you to avoid long lines at the airport. Print your boarding pass or save it to your mobile device for quick access.

Security Screening: Prepare for security screenings. Remove liquids and electronics from your carry-on and deposit in the designated bins. Follow security officers' instructions and be patient; they are simply doing their jobs to keep everyone safe.

Airport amenities typically include shops, restaurants, and lounges. Take advantage of these amenities to make your wait more bearable. Grab a snack or a book to read on the plane.

On the flight

Comfort: For a more comfortable journey, bring a travel pillow, noise-canceling headphones, and a favorite book or soundtrack. Air travel may be exhausting, so keeping yourself comfortable is essential.

Hydration: airplane cabins can be dry, so drink plenty of water when flying. Avoid drinking too much caffeine or alcohol, as both can cause dehydration.

Arrival Information: Keep an eye out for announcements regarding your arrival time and gate. Check the in-flight entertainment for information on local time in Thessaloniki, so you can change your watch and prepare for landing.

Arrival in Thessaloniki

Immigration & Customs

Immigration Control: When you arrive at Macedonia Airport, follow the signs to immigration. Have your passport and any required visas ready for examination. If you are a tourist, you will normally only need to provide your passport and potential proof of future travel.

Customs: After clearing immigration, go to Customs. Declare any objects you're bringing into the nation that may require declaration, such as substantial amounts of cash or commercial goods. Most travelers will pass through customs quickly.

Airport Transfer Options (Taxi, Shuttle, and Public Transportation):

Taxis:

Taxis are readily available at Thessaloniki Airport. Follow the instructions for the taxi stand outside the terminal. To prevent being overcharged, make sure you utilize official cabs.

Taxi rates to central Thessaloniki are typically fixed or computed by meter. The trip takes roughly 30 minutes, depending on traffic. Before you leave, request an estimate from the driver.

Shuttles:

Airport Shuttle Services: Thessaloniki Airport provides shuttle services to a variety of destinations. Check ahead of time to see whether your hotel offers an airport shuttle or if

There are shuttle services that will take you directly to your accommodation.

Public Transportation:

Bus: Public buses connect the airport to Thessaloniki's core and other places. The number 78 and 78N (night service) buses run often and are an inexpensive choice. Bus stops are provided right outside the terminal. Tickets can be purchased at kiosks or directly from the driver.

Train: While there is no direct train link from the airport, Thessaloniki's main train station (Kentriki Stathmos) is easily accessible by bus or cab if you intend to travel further by train.

Professional tips for a smooth arrival

Currency Exchange: If you need to convert money, there are currency exchange kiosks available at the airport. However, the rates may not be the best, so withdraw cash from ATMs or use credit/debit cards.

SIM Cards: You can get a local SIM card for your phone at the airport or in the city. Having local data and a phone connection can be really convenient.

Local Information: Get a city map or a travel brochure from the airport's information desk. This can provide essential information about public transportation, tourist attractions, and local contacts.

Stay Connected: Download key travel apps like maps, translation tools, and local transportation apps to stay connected and easily around Thessaloniki.

With these ideas and information, your trip to Thessaloniki should run as smoothly as a well-oiled Greek olive oil mill. These tips will help you get through the airport and into this amazing city with minimal fuss and maximum excitement, whether you're from nearby or far away. Travel safely and enjoy every bit of your Thessaloniki adventure.

CHAPTER THREE

Getting Around Thessaloniki

Welcome to Thessaloniki, where the city's vibrant streets and lively neighborhoods invite you to explore. This charming city is fun to navigate, and knowing your options can help. From hopping on a bus to strolling through historic quarters, this guide will help you navigate Thessaloniki like a pro.

Local Transportation

Thessaloniki is a city that embraces both its rich history and modern conveniences, and its local transportation system is designed to make your journey as smooth as possible. Whether you're aiming to explore ancient ruins or savor local delicacies, knowing how to get around is key to unlocking all that this city has to offer.

Buses

Overview:

Thessaloniki's bus network is extensive and offers an economical way to get around the city. Operated by the **Thessaloniki Public Transport Organization (OASTH)**, The buses cover a broad range of routes, connecting key areas including the city center, neighborhoods, and the outskirts.

How to Use:

- **Tickets:** Before boarding, you'll need to purchase a ticket. You can buy tickets from kiosks, OASTH ticket offices, or even on the bus, though the latter option may be less convenient. Ticket prices are generally affordable, with single-ride tickets costing around €1.20. Make sure to validate your ticket upon boarding by stamping it at the machine located near the bus door.

- **Routes:** Buses are numbered, and route information is displayed on the front of the bus. The OASTH website and mobile app provide up-to-date route maps and schedules. Key routes include those that connect the airport to the city center, as well as popular routes like number 1, which circles the city.
- **Timing:** Buses run frequently throughout the day, with most routes operating from early morning until late evening. For specific schedules, check the OASTH website or app, especially if you plan to travel during off-peak hours.

Pro Tips:

- **Be on Time:** Buses can be punctual, so arriving a few minutes early can ensure you don't miss your ride.
- **Plan Ahead:** Use the OASTH app or website to plan your journey and get real-time updates on bus arrivals and delays.

Trams

Overview:

Thessaloniki's tram system offers a scenic and leisurely way to navigate the city, especially along the waterfront. Though it covers fewer areas than buses, it's perfect for enjoying the city's beautiful views while traveling.

How to Use:

- **Tickets:** Tram tickets are the same as bus tickets and can be purchased from kiosks or vending machines. A single ticket costs around €1.20, and you must validate it before boarding.
- **Routes:** The tram network is less extensive than the bus system, but it covers popular routes such as those connecting the waterfront and key parts of the city. Check the route maps available at tram stops or online.
- **Timing:** Trams run from early morning until late evening, but they are less frequent than buses. Check the tram schedules in advance to avoid long waits.

Pro Tips:

- **Enjoy the Ride:** Trams offer excellent views of the city, especially along the waterfront. Sit back and enjoy the scenic journey.
- **Check Schedules:** Trams can be less frequent, so it's wise to check departure times in advance.

Taxis

Overview:

Taxis in Thessaloniki offer a convenient and comfortable way to travel, especially if you're carrying luggage or prefer door-to-door service. They're also handy for reaching destinations that are less accessible by public transport.

How to Use:

- **Hailing a Taxi:** Taxis can be hailed on the street or booked by phone. You'll recognize them by their yellow color and taxi sign. They can also be found at designated taxi stands throughout the city.
- Taxis operate on a meter system, with base fares starting around €3.50 and additional charges based on distance and time. There may be extra fees for luggage or late-night rides.
- **Payment:** Most taxis accept cash and credit cards, but it's always a beneficial idea to confirm payment methods with the driver before starting your journey.

Pro Tips:

- **Confirm the Fare:** Before starting your ride, ask the driver for an estimate or check the meter to avoid surprises.
- **Book in Advance:** For convenience, especially during peak hours, consider booking a taxi in advance.

Bicycle Rentals

Overview:

Thessaloniki is becoming increasingly bike-friendly, with dedicated bike lanes and bike rental services available throughout the city. Renting a bicycle is a great way to explore at your own pace and enjoy the fresh air.

How to Use:

- **Rental Services:** Several companies provide bicycle rentals, including Bike4Fun and Thessaloniki Bike. Rental stations are located in popular areas, including the waterfront and city center.
- **Pricing:** Rental prices are generally reasonable, with options for hourly, daily, or weekly rentals. Helmets and locks are typically included, but always check what's provided before you rent.
- **Bike Lanes:** Thessaloniki has dedicated bike lanes and routes, particularly along the waterfront and in central areas. Follow traffic rules and be mindful of pedestrians.

Pro Tips:

- **Safety First:** When leaving your bike unattended, always wear a helmet and use a bike lock.

- **Plan Your Route:** Familiarize yourself with bike-friendly routes and traffic conditions to ensure a smooth ride.

Walking

Overview:

Walking is one of the best ways to experience Thessaloniki, especially in the compact city center. Many of the city's attractions, cafes, and shops are within walking distance, making it a delightful way to explore.

How to Enjoy Walking:

- **City Center:** The city center is pedestrian-friendly, with wide sidewalks and plenty of pedestrian crossings. Explore areas like Aristotelous Square, the waterfront promenade, and Ano Poli (the Old Town) on foot.
- **Walking Tours:** Consider joining a guided walking tour to learn more about Thessaloniki's history and culture. Many tours cover key landmarks and offer insider tips.
- **Comfortable Shoes:** Since you'll be doing a lot of walking, wear comfortable shoes and bring a reusable water bottle to stay hydrated.

Pro Tips:

- **Get Lost:** Don't be afraid to wander off the beaten path. Thessaloniki's charm often lies in its lesser-known streets and local neighborhoods.
- **Map It Out:** While getting lost can be fun, having a map or navigation app can help you find your way back if needed.

Navigating the City

Navigating Thessaloniki is a blend of modern convenience and historic charm. Whether you're hopping on a bus, taking a tram, or exploring on foot, the city's layout and transportation options make getting around relatively easy.

Tips for Easy Navigation:

- **City Layout:** Thessaloniki's city center is compact and organized around key areas like Aristotelous Square and the waterfront. Major landmarks are well-signed, making it easier to find your way.
- **Public Transport Apps:** Utilize apps for public transport schedules, route planning, and real-time updates. The OASTH app is particularly useful for checking bus and tram routes.

- **Local Assistance:** Don't hesitate to ask locals for directions or recommendations. Thessaloniki's residents are friendly and often eager to assist.
- When navigating the city, use major landmarks such as the White Tower or the Rotunda as reference points. They're not only significant historical sites but also great navigation aids.

Exploring Beyond the City Center:

- **Day Trips:** If you plan to explore areas outside the city, such as the Halkidiki peninsula or nearby villages, consider renting a car or using organized tours. Public transport options may be limited in these areas.
- **Cultural insights:** visit neighborhood markets, traditional taverns, and local festivals to embrace the local culture. Walking through these areas provides a deeper understanding of Thessaloniki's character.

With these insights into Thessaloniki's transportation options and city navigation, you're well-equipped to explore every corner of this dynamic city. Whether you're hopping on a bus, renting a bike, or simply strolling through its vibrant streets, Thessaloniki is sure to enchant you at every turn. Enjoy the journey, and let the city's charm guide your adventure!

CHAPTER FOUR

Accommodation

Finding the perfect place to stay is like choosing the right seasoning for a dish—it can make all the difference. Thessaloniki offers a diverse range of accommodation options, catering to different tastes, budgets, and needs. From luxurious hotels to cozy guesthouses and practical hostels, there's something for every traveler.

Types of Accommodations

Hotels

Hotels in Thessaloniki range from opulent five-star establishments to charming boutique hotels, each offering a unique experience. Here's a roundup of some top choices across different categories:

1. **Electra Palace Thessaloniki**
   - **Overview:** A luxurious five-star hotel located in the heart of the city, offering stunning views of the city and the sea. Features include a rooftop pool, spa, and gourmet restaurant.
   - **Price Range:** €150-€300 per night
   - **Location:** Aristotelous 9, Thessaloniki 546 24, Greece.
   - **Safety:** The hotel has high security standards with 24/7 surveillance and in-room safes.
2. **Makedonia Palace**
   - **Overview:** Known for its elegance and high-end service, Makedonia Palace offers luxurious rooms and suites with panoramic views of the Thermaic Gulf. It includes a fitness center and fine dining.
   - **Price Range:** €200-€350 per night

- **Location:** Leoforos Megalou Alexandrou 2, Thessaloniki 546 40 Greece, near the waterfront.
- **Safety:** Well-secured, with modern safety measures and a safe environment.

3. **The Modernist Thessaloniki**
   - **Overview:** A chic, modern boutique hotel featuring sleek design and personalized service. It offers an artistic vibe and is popular among design enthusiasts.
   - **Price Range:** €120-€200 per night
   - **Location:** Ermou 32, Thessaloniki 54623, near the city center
   - **Safety:** A safe neighborhood with a secure entry system and concierge service.

4. **Hotel Victoria**
   - **Overview:** A well-maintained three-star hotel known for its affordability and central location. It offers comfortable rooms and a complimentary breakfast.
   - **Price Range:** €52-€120 per night
   - **Location:** 13 Langada Street, Thessaloniki, close to major attractions.
   - **Safety:** Safe, with a good reputation, but it's always good to stay alert in busy areas.

5. **City Hotel Thessaloniki**

- **Overview:** A stylish four-star hotel offering contemporary design and a central location. Features include a rooftop bar and modern amenities.
- **Price Range:** €100-€180 per night
- **Location:** 11 Komninon St.., Thessaloniki 54624 , near the train station
- **Safety:** Secure with good reviews on safety and comfort.

6. **Park Hotel**
   - **Overview:** A classic option with spacious rooms and a central location. The hotel provides a satisfactory balance between comfort and price.
   - **Price Range:** €90-€150 per night
   - **Location:** 81 Ionos Dragoumi Str. 54630, Thessaloniki.
   - **Safety:** Generally safe, with a focus on guest comfort and security.

7. **Le Palace Art Hotel**
   - **Overview:** A boutique hotel blending modern amenities with historical charm. It features art-themed decor and a prime location.
   - **Price Range:** €120-€180 per night
   - **Location:** Tsimiski 12, Thessaloniki 546 24, Greece.

- Safety: Safe, with a high level of customer
    service and security.

Hostels

For those traveling on a budget or seeking a more social atmosphere, Thessaloniki's hostels offer an affordable and fun option. Here are some recommended hostels:

Stay Hybrid Hotel

- **Overview**: Modern and social with both dormitory and private rooms, plus a communal kitchen.
- **Price Range**: €20-€50 per night
- **Location**: 61 Ionos Dragoumi Str. 54630, Thessaloniki.
- **Safety**: Individual lockers, 24/7 reception, and good reviews for cleanliness and security.

Kamara Hostel (RentRooms Thessaloniki)

- **Overview**: cozy, budget-friendly hostel with basic amenities.
- **Price Range**: €15-€35 per night
- **Location**:—Dim. Gounari 51, Thessaloniki 54621, Greece (right next to the Kamara Arch, hence the name).

- **Safety**: Located in a safe area near the university, well-reviewed for cleanliness and security.

The wanderlust hostel

- **Overview**: Community-driven hostel with a laid-back vibe, communal lounge, and events.
- **Price Range**: €22-€55 per night
- **Location**: Athanasiou Diakou 1, Thessaloniki 55438, Greece.
- **Safety**: 24/7 staff and individual lockers for security, well-rated for friendliness and a safe environment.

Jetpak Alternative

- **Overview**: Practical, no-frills hostel with central location and free Wi-Fi.
- **Price Range**: €18-€40 per night
- **Location**: Siggrou 15, Thessaloniki 54630, Greece (close to the city center).
- **Safety**: safe with keycard access and attentive staff.

Atlas City Hostel

- **Price Range**: €19-€50 per night
- **Location**: 40 Egnatia St., Thessaloniki 54625, Greece
- **Number of Rooms**: 31 rooms

- **Safety**: Modern safety features, including 24/7 reception and personal lockers, ensure security. Located centrally, providing easy access to nearby attractions like Aristotelous Square

Guesshouse in Thessaloniki

Avenue Hotel

- **Price Range**: €60-€120 per night
- **Rooms**: 12 rooms, each with modern amenities
- **Safety**: Located in a safe neighborhood with 24-hour front desk service.
- **Proximity**: Close to Aristotelous Square, only a 10-15 minute walk from the city's main attractions.

Lena's Guesthouse

- **Price Range**: €50-€90 per night
- **Rooms**: 8 cozy rooms with a homely feel
- **Safety**: Safe area with attentive staff and personal lockers.
- **Proximity**: About 20 minutes on foot from the White Tower and other key sights.

House on the Hill

- **Price Range**: €50-€100 per night

- **Rooms**: 10 rooms with stunning views of the city.
- **Safety**: high guest reviews for security and peaceful environment.
- **Proximity**: Situated in Ano Poli, it's close to traditional tavernas and offers views over Thessaloniki.

Aristotelous Guesthouse

- **Price Range**: €65-€130 per night
- **Rooms**: 15 spacious rooms
- **Safety**: Centrally located with good security features and reviews.
- **Proximity**: In Aristotelous Square, within walking distance of the Rotunda, White Tower, and other major attractions.

Bella Vista Guesthouse

- **Price Range**: €60-€110 per night
- **Rooms**: 12 rooms offering panoramic views.
- **Safety**: Secure with modern safety measures in place.
- **Proximity**: A short walk to the city center and Ladadika district, famous for its nightlife.

Old Town Guesthouse

- **Price Range**: €70-€120 per night

- **Rooms**: 10 rooms
- **Safety**: Located in a quiet, historic area with secure facilities.
- **Proximity**: Close to Ano Poli and only 15-20 minutes away from the city center's main attractions.

The Modern Guesthouse

- **Price Range**: €80-€150 per night
- **Rooms**: 14 rooms with modern furnishings.
- **Safety**: Good reviews for security, located in a quiet, upscale area.
- **Proximity**: Near the Modiano Market and Ladadika, a 10-minute walk to the heart of the city.

Central House Thessaloniki

- **Price Range**: €55-€110 per night
- **Rooms**: 9 rooms
- **Safety**: Located in a central but quiet area, ensuring security.
- **Proximity**: Within 5 minutes from major attractions like the White Tower and the Thessaloniki Archaeological Museum.

Thessaloniki Delight

- **Price Range**: €75-€120 per night

- **Rooms**: 12 rooms
- **Safety**: Located in a safe area near the waterfront with good security.
- **Proximity**: Close to the city center and waterfront, making it easy to explore the city's main attractions on foot.

Cozy Guesthouse

- **Price Range**: €65-€110 per night
- **Rooms**: 10 rooms
- **Safety**: secure entry system and helpful staff.
- **Proximity**: Located near the Ano Poli district, known for its traditional architecture and easy access to historical sites.

Apartment

Luxury Living Apartments

- Overview: Offers upscale apartments with modern amenities, perfect for travelers seeking high-end accommodations.
- Price Range: €80-€200 per night
- Location: Close to Aristotelous Square, central Thessaloniki.
- Safety: Secured with modern keycard systems and well-reviewed for safety.

Petite Palace Aristotelous 7

- Overview: A well-located, budget-friendly option, offering charming apartments close to key attractions like the White Tower.
- Price Range: €60-€120 per night
- Location: Aristotelous Square, Thessaloniki.
- Safety: Known for being in a central and safe neighborhood.

Julie's Sunshine Apartment

- Overview: cozy and family-friendly, with easy access to the Arch of Galerius and White Tower.
- Price Range: €80-€150 per night
- Location: Ippodromiou Square.
- Safety: The apartment enjoys a good safety reputation and is located in a popular tourist area.

Panorama View Apartment

- Overview: A luxurious option located in the Panorama district, offering scenic views and a serene environment.
- Price Range: €90-€170 per night
- Location: Panorama district.
- Safety: Well-regarded for its quiet and safe location.

White Tower 1 Bedroom Apartment

- Overview: A well-equipped, affordable apartment near the White Tower, perfect for those wanting to explore Thessaloniki's historic sites.
- Price Range: €50-€100 per night
- Location: Near the White Tower, Thessaloniki.
- Safety: Located in a safe, tourist-friendly area.

Dimitris House 3

- Overview: A spacious apartment, ideal for families, located near the White Tower and other cultural landmarks.
- Price Range: €55-€130 per night
- Location: Near the White Tower and Roman Agora.
- Safety: The area is considered safe for tourists, with positive reviews on safety measures.

Central Luxury Apartments

- Overview: Modern and stylish apartments located in the city center, offering great access to the waterfront and local dining.
- Price Range: €100-€250 per night
- Location: Close to the promenade and central squares.
- Safety: Features high-end security and excellent guest reviews.

Recommended Areas to Stay

Choosing the right area can significantly enhance your Thessaloniki experience. Here are some recommended neighborhoods:

City Center

- **Safety**: This area is very central, with high foot traffic and a heavy police presence, making it one of the safest parts of the city. It's convenient for tourists, with many hotels, shops, and restaurants. However, as in any busy area, be mindful of pickpockets in crowded spaces.
- **Recommendation**: Ideal for travelers who want easy access to Thessaloniki's main attractions.

Ladadika

- **Safety**: Ladadika is known for its nightlife, so it's generally safe but can get crowded and loud, especially during the night. Like any nightlife area, it's wise to remain cautious after dark.
- **Recommendation**: Perfect for those who want to enjoy Thessaloniki's vibrant evening scene. Solo travelers should take usual safety precautions.

Ano Poli (Old Town)

- **Safety**: This area is quieter and offers a more traditional vibe, with narrow streets and fewer crowds. It's generally very safe, but as with most quiet areas, it's better to avoid walking alone late at night.
- **Recommendation**: Great for those seeking a peaceful stay with beautiful views and historical charm.

Waterfront (Nea Paralia)

- **Safety**: Nea Paralia is very safe, well-lit, and ideal for scenic walks along the sea. The area is popular among locals and tourists alike, making it a pleasant and secure place to stay.
- **Recommendation**: Best for those who enjoy relaxing environments with easy access to outdoor spaces and the sea.

Kamara

- **Safety**: Kamara is a lively area, especially around the Arch of Galerius, and is generally safe. It's a favorite meeting spot for locals and tourists, so expect crowds during the day.
- **Recommendation**: Ideal for those who want to be close to historical landmarks and the city's vibrant life.

Modiano Market Area

- **Safety**: While this area is bustling during the day, it can be quieter at night when the market closes. As always, staying aware of your surroundings in busy market areas is recommended.
- **Recommendation**: Great for food lovers and those who want a lively, urban vibe during the day. Some caution is needed at night due to quieter streets.

Valaoritou

- **Safety**: Valaoritou is a trendy area known for its bars and nightlife, which means it can get busy and noisy in the evenings. Like Ladadika, it's safe but crowded, and late-night travelers should take usual precautions.
- **Recommendation**: Perfect for younger travelers or those looking for a lively, modern neighborhood.

Safety

Thessaloniki is generally a safe city for travelers, but like any urban area, it's important to stay vigilant. Here are some safety tips:

- **Secure Your Belongings:** Use hotel safes or secure lockers in hostels to keep your valuables safe.

- **Stay Aware:** Be cautious in crowded areas and avoid displaying expensive items or large amounts of cash.
- **Emergency Contacts:** Familiarize yourself with local emergency contacts and the location of the nearest hospital or police station.
- **Local Advice:** Don't hesitate to ask hotel or hostel staff for advice on safe areas and local customs.

Whether you're seeking luxury, budget-friendly options, or something in between, Thessaloniki's diverse range of accommodations ensures that you'll find the perfect place to stay. From elegant hotels and social hostels to charming guesthouses and fully equipped apartments, each option offers its own unique experience. By choosing the right place to stay and exploring the city's various neighborhoods, you'll be well on your way to an unforgettable adventure in Thessaloniki. Enjoy your stay, and may your time in this vibrant city be filled with comfort, exploration, and delightful discoveries!

CHAPTER FIVE

Exploring Thessaloniki

Thessaloniki, Greece's vibrant second city, is a treasure trove of history, culture, and stunning sights. Whether you're wandering through ancient ruins, marveling at modern architecture, or soaking in breathtaking views, Thessaloniki has something to captivate every traveler. In this chapter, we'll delve into the top attractions, historical sites, modern landmarks, scenic viewpoints, churches and monasteries, and museums and galleries that make Thessaloniki an unforgettable destination.

Top Attractions

1. White Tower

Overview: The White Tower is the most recognizable symbol of Thessaloniki. It was originally built as a Byzantine fortification in the 12th century, but it has undergone various transformations over the centuries. It served as a fortress, a prison, and even a lighthouse before becoming a museum. Today, it houses exhibits about the city's history and provides panoramic views of Thessaloniki and the Thermaic Gulf.

History: The White Tower was constructed by the Byzantine Emperor Isaac II Angelos as part of the city's fortifications. During the Ottoman period, it was known as the "Tower of Blood" due to its use as a prison where many executions occurred. It was restored and converted into a museum in the 20th century.

How to Navigate: The White Tower is located on the waterfront along the city's promenade. It's easily accessible by public transportation, including buses and taxis. From

Aristotelous Square, you can walk along the waterfront for about 15 minutes to reach the tower.

Prices:

- **Admission Fee:** approximately €6 for adults, with reduced prices for students and seniors. Free admission on certain days of the year.
- **Opening Hours:** Typically open from 8:00 AM to 8:00 PM, with extended hours in peak tourist season.

Fun to experience: Climbing to the top of the White Tower offers one of the best views of Thessaloniki. The exhibits inside provide a fascinating look into the city's history with artifacts and interactive displays. The panoramic view from the observation deck is a wonderful spot for photography, especially at sunset.

2. Aristotelous Square

Overview: Aristotelous Square is the heart of Thessaloniki, a grand open space lined with impressive neoclassical buildings. It's the city's main gathering place, hosting public events, festivals, and markets. The square is surrounded by cafes, shops, and restaurants, making it a vibrant spot for visitors.

History: The square was designed by the French architect Ernest Hébrard in the early 20th century as part of the city's reconstruction after the great fire of 1917. Its design reflects the city's desire to embrace modernity while preserving its historical essence.

How to Navigate: Located in the city center, Aristotelous Square is easily reachable by foot from various parts of Thessaloniki. It's also well served by public transportation, including buses and taxis. The square is a hub for both local and tourist activities.

Prices:

- **Admission Fee:** Free to access.
- **Opening Hours:** Always open, as it's a public space.

Fun to Experience: Aristotelous Square is perfect for people-watching and enjoying the city's lively atmosphere. The surrounding cafes and restaurants offer a great spot to relax and soak in the ambiance. Public events and festivals often take place here, adding to the square's vibrant energy.

3. Rotunda

Overview: The rotunda is a massive round structure with a rich history. Originally built as a mausoleum for Emperor Galerius in the 4th century AD, it was later converted into a church and then a mosque. Today, it's a UNESCO World Heritage Site and a museum showcasing its transformation over the centuries.

History: The Rotunda was commissioned by Emperor Galerius as a mausoleum for himself but was never used for this purpose. It was converted into a Christian church dedicated to Saint George and later into a mosque during the Ottoman era. Its architecture and decorations reveal its historical layers.

How to Navigate: The Rotunda is located near the Arch of Galerius, not far from Aristotelous Square. It's easily accessible on foot or by public transport. Buses and taxis frequently pass by this area.

Prices:

- **Admission Fee:** Approximately €4 for adults.
- **Opening Hours:** Typically open from 8:00 AM to 3:00 PM.

Fun to Experience: The Rotunda's massive dome and

intricate mosaics are awe-inspiring. Its transformation from a mausoleum to a church and mosque provides a fascinating glimpse into Thessaloniki's diverse history. The building's sheer size and architectural beauty make it a must-visit.

4. Ano Poli (Old Town)

Overview: Ano Poli, or the Old Town, is a historic neighborhood that survived the great fire of 1917. It's characterized by its traditional houses, narrow streets, and stunning views of the city. Ano Poli offers a glimpse into Thessaloniki's past and is known for its charming atmosphere.

History: Ano Poli is one of the few areas in Thessaloniki that retained its traditional architecture after the fire. The neighborhood reflects the city's Ottoman and Byzantine heritage, with its old houses and narrow streets.

How to Navigate: Ano Poli is located on the hills north of the city center. It's accessible by bus, taxi, or on foot. Walking through its winding streets is a great way to explore the area and discover its hidden gems.

Prices:

- **Admission fee:** Free to explore.

Fun to Experience: Strolling through Ano Poli is like stepping back in time. The neighborhood's traditional houses and narrow alleys are perfect for exploring on foot. There are several quaint tavernas where you can enjoy traditional Greek cuisine while taking in panoramic views of the city.

5. Ladadika District

Overview: Ladadika is a historic district that has become a vibrant nightlife hub. Known for its colorful buildings and traditional tavernas, it's a popular area for dining, drinking, and enjoying live music.

History: Ladadika was historically a commercial area where olive oil was traded. In recent decades, it has undergone a transformation into a lively district with a mix of modern and traditional elements.

How to Navigate: Located near the waterfront and the city center, Ladadika is easily accessible by foot, bus, or taxi. It's a short walk from Aristotelous Square.

Prices:

- **Admission fee:** Free to explore.

Fun to Experience: Ladadika comes alive in the evenings with its bustling bars and restaurants. It's a great place to enjoy a night out with live music, traditional Greek dishes, and a vibrant atmosphere.

6. Modiano Market

Overview: Modiano Market is a bustling covered market where you can experience the local flavors of Thessaloniki.

It's filled with stalls selling fresh produce, meats, fish, and local delicacies.

History: Opened in the early 20th century, Modiano Market is named after the Jewish architect Eli Modiano, who designed the market. It reflects the city's rich cultural and commercial history.

How to Navigate: The market is located in the city center, near Aristotelous Square. It's easily reachable by foot or by public transport. Buses and taxis frequently pass by the area.

Prices:

- **Admission Fee:** Free to enter.

Fun to Experience: Walking through Modiano Market is a sensory delight. The vibrant colors and aromas of fresh produce and local specialties create a lively atmosphere. It's a wonderful place to sample local foods and experience the city's culinary culture.

7. Thessaloniki Waterfront (Nea Paralia)

Overview: The Thessaloniki Waterfront, or Nea Paralia, is a beautifully developed promenade that stretches along the Thermaic Gulf. It's an ideal place for leisurely walks, jogging, or relaxing by the sea.

History: The waterfront was transformed in the early 2000s as part of an urban development project to enhance the city's coastline and create a recreational space for residents and visitors.

How to Navigate: The promenade stretches from the White Tower to the port area. It's easily accessible by foot, bike, or public transport. Many buses and taxis serve the waterfront area.

Prices:

- **Admission Fee:** Free to access.

Fun to Experience: The Thessaloniki Waterfront offers stunning views of the sea and the city's skyline. It's a great place for a leisurely stroll, especially at sunset. The promenade also features parks, cultural installations, and outdoor cafes.

8. Heptapyrgion (Yedi Kule)

Overview: Heptapyrgion, also known as Yedi Kule, is a Byzantine fortress situated on the hills overlooking Thessaloniki. It offers historical insights and panoramic views of the city.

History: The fortress was originally built by the Byzantines to protect the city. It was later used as a prison during the

Ottoman period. Today, it stands as a historical monument offering a glimpse into the city's past.

How to Navigate: Heptapyrgion is located on the eastern hills of Thessaloniki. It's accessible by bus, taxi, or on foot. The hike up to the fortress provides a chance to enjoy panoramic views of the city.

Prices:

- **Admission Fee:** Approximately €3 for adults.
- **Opening Hours:** Typically open from 8:00 AM to 3:00 PM.

Fun to Experience: Exploring Heptapyrgion provides a fascinating look at the city's medieval fortifications. The fortress's panoramic views are spectacular, making it an ideal spot for photography and enjoying the cityscape.

9. Saint Demetrius Church (Agios Dimitrios)

Overview: The Church of Saint Demetrius is one of Thessaloniki's most significant religious sites, dedicated to the city's patron saint, Saint Demetrius. It's known for its beautiful mosaics and historical artifacts.

History: Built in the 7th century, the church was constructed over the remains of an earlier basilica. For centuries, it has been an important pilgrimage site and remains a central place of worship in Thessaloniki.

How to Navigate: The church is located in the city center, near the Roman Agora. It's easily accessible by foot, bus, or taxi from various parts of the city.

Prices:

- **Admission Fee:** Free to enter, though donations are appreciated.
- **Opening Hours:** Typically open from 7:00 AM to 8:00 PM.

Fun to Experience: The church's stunning mosaics and architectural details are a highlight. It's a peaceful place to explore and reflect, with historical artifacts and religious relics adding to its significance.

10. Galerius Arch (Kamara)

Overview: The Galerius Arch, or Kamara, is a triumphal arch built by Emperor Galerius to commemorate his victory over the Persians. It's located near the Rotunda and is known for its impressive Roman reliefs.

History: The arch was constructed in the early 4th century AD and is one of the best-preserved Roman monuments in

Thessaloniki. It was originally part of a larger complex that included the Rotunda and a palace.

How to Navigate: The arch is located in the city center, near the Rotunda. It's easily accessible on foot or by public transport. Buses and taxis frequently pass by this historical site.

Prices:

- **Admission Fee:** Free to access.
- **Opening Hours: The public monument is always open.**

Fun to Experience: The Galerius Arch is a great place to appreciate Roman art and architecture. The detailed reliefs depicting Galerius's victories are fascinating, and the arch itself is a significant historical landmark.

11. Archaeological Museum of Thessaloniki

Overview: The Archaeological Museum of Thessaloniki houses a vast collection of artifacts from Macedonia, including sculptures, pottery, and ancient jewelry. It's one of the most important archaeological museums in Greece.

History: Established in the early 20th century, the museum's collection spans from prehistoric times to the Byzantine period. It showcases the rich cultural heritage of Macedonia and its influence on Greek history.

How to Navigate: The museum is located near the city center, not far from the White Tower. It's easily reachable by foot, taxi, or bus.

Prices:

- **Admission Fee:** Approximately €8 for adults, with reduced rates for students and seniors.
- **Opening Hours:** Typically open from 8:00 AM to 8:00 PM.

Fun to Experience: The museum's extensive collection offers a deep dive into Macedonia's history. The exhibits are well-curated, providing insights into ancient Greek civilization through sculptures, artifacts, and interactive displays.

12. Byzantine Walls

Overview: The Byzantine Walls of Thessaloniki are ancient fortifications that once encircled the city. Sections of these walls still stand today, offering a glimpse into the city's defensive past.

History: Built in the 4th century AD, the walls were constructed to protect Thessaloniki from invasions. Over the centuries, they were expanded and reinforced, reflecting the city's changing needs for defense.

How to Navigate: The walls are spread across various parts of the city, with several access points. They are best explored on foot, and walking along the walls provides panoramic views of Thessaloniki.

Prices:

- **Admission Fee:** Free to access.

Fun to Experience: Walking along the Byzantine Walls offers a unique perspective on the city's history. The views from the walls are excellent for photography, and the historical significance adds to the experience.

13. Museum of Byzantine Culture

Overview: The Museum of Byzantine Culture is dedicated to Byzantine art and culture, showcasing an extensive collection of artifacts from the Byzantine period. It's one of the most important museums in Greece dedicated to Byzantine history.

History: Founded in the late 20th century, the museum aims to preserve and display the rich cultural heritage of the Byzantine Empire. Its collection includes mosaics, icons, and religious artifacts.

How to Navigate: Located in the city center, the museum is easily accessible by public transport, taxi, or on foot.

Prices:

- **Admission Fee:** Approximately €8 for adults, with reduced rates for students and seniors.
- **Opening Hours:** Typically open from 8:00 AM to 8:00 PM.

Fun to Experience: The museum's collection provides a comprehensive overview of Byzantine art and culture. The exhibits are well presented, offering insights into the religious and artistic practices of the Byzantine Empire.

14. Thessaloniki Concert Hall (Macedonia Palace)

Overview: The Thessaloniki Concert Hall, also known as Macedonia Palace, is a modern cultural venue hosting a variety of performances, including concerts, theater, and dance.

History: Opened in the early 2000s, the concert hall is a state-of-the-art facility designed to enhance Thessaloniki's cultural scene. It hosts a range of events throughout the year.

How to Navigate: Located near the waterfront, the concert hall is accessible by public transport, taxi, or on foot from the city center.

Prices:

- **Admission Fee:** Varies depending on the event.
- **Opening Hours:** Varies depending on the performance schedule.

Fun to Experience: Attending a performance at the Thessaloniki Concert Hall is a great way to experience the city's vibrant cultural scene. The modern facility provides excellent acoustics and a comfortable environment for enjoying a wide range of performances.

15. Olympos Theater

Overview: The Olympos Theater is an ancient theater used for performances during the Roman period. It offers insights into Thessaloniki's ancient cultural life and is an important archaeological site.

History: Constructed in the 2nd century AD, the theater was used for various performances and events. It reflects the city's role as a major cultural center during the Roman Empire.

How to Navigate: Located near the city center, the theater is easily accessible by foot or by public transport. It's situated close to other historical sites, making it a convenient stop on a historical tour.

Prices:

- **Admission Fee:** Free to access.

Fun to Experience: Exploring the Olympos Theater provides a glimpse into ancient Thessaloniki's cultural life. The ruins offer a fascinating look at Roman-era architecture and provide a peaceful spot for reflection and photography.

Historical Sites

1. Roman: During the Roman era, the Roman Forum of Thessaloniki, also known as the Forum of Thessalonica, served as the city's civic and commercial heart. The site includes the remnants of stores, public baths, and a basilica, providing a look into the city's vibrant history.

History: The Roman Forum, built in the second century AD, was the focal point of public life in Thessaloniki. It housed a basilica for Christian gatherings, public baths for socializing, and a marketplace for trade. The forum reflects on the role of public places in Roman urban planning and daily life.

How to get there: The Roman Forum is in the city center, easily accessible on foot from Aristotelous Square or by public transportation. It is located near the intersection of Egnatia and Vasileos Irakliou Streets.

What to Do:

Explore the Ruins: Walk through the forum's remnants, looking at the shops, the public bath, and the basilica.

Visit the Museum: An on-site museum offers in-depth descriptions of the site's history and artifacts unearthed during excavations.

Prices:

Admission costs approximately €6 for adults.
Opening hours are typically from 8:00 a.m. to 3:00 p.m. daily. Check for seasonal changes or unusual closings.

The Roman Forum provides an intriguing glimpse into the ancient city's public and social life. The well-preserved remains and educational exhibits make it an intriguing destination for history buffs.

2. Thessaloniki's Agora served as the city's main marketplace and municipal center. The site contains the remnants of several public buildings and streets, which depict the city's commercial and administrative heart.

History: The Agora, founded in the third century BC, served as a hub for economic, political, and social activities. It was surrounded by significant public structures, including administrative offices and temples. The Agora's layout reveals much about ancient Greek urban planning and public life.

How to get there: The Agora is conveniently located near the Roman Forum and can be reached by foot or public transportation from the city center. It's located on Egnatia Street.

What to Do:

Explore the website: Wander among the remnants of historic structures and streets.

Learn from the exhibits: The complex has informative panels and sometimes guided walks that explain the importance of various structures.

Prices:

Admission costs approximately €6 for adults.
Opening hours are typically from 8:00 a.m. to 3:00 p.m. daily.
Check the current hours of operation before visiting.

The Agora offers a realistic representation of ancient Thessaloniki's economic and political life. The open-air ruins and historical background make for an intriguing visit.

3. Ancient Odeon Overview: The Ancient Odeon is a Roman theater in Thessaloniki with outstanding preservation. It is used for performances and public events, with well-maintained seating and staging areas.

History: Built in the second century AD, the Odeon was intended for musical performances and dramatic activities. It is an excellent example of Roman entertainment architecture, evoking the cultural significance of public performances in antiquity.

How to get there: The Odeon is located near the downtown of Thessaloniki and may be accessed on foot from Aristotelous Square or by public transportation. It is located at the corner of Egnatia and Karytsi streets.

What to Do:

Explore the theater: Walk through the seating area and stage, imagining the performances that took place there.

Attend Events: Look for any special performances or events that may be happening at the Odeon.

Prices:

Admission costs approximately €6 for adults.
Opening hours are typically from 8:00 a.m. to 3:00 p.m. daily.

Fun Factor: The Ancient Odeon provides a physical link to the city's Roman history. Its well-preserved ruins create a dramatic backdrop for studying ancient entertainment.

4. Eptapyrgio Stronghold Overview: This Byzantine-era stronghold, also known as YediKule, provides historical insights and panoramic views over Thessaloniki. The name "Eptapyrgio" means "Seven Towers," which reflects the defensive arrangement.

History: The fortress, built in the 12th century, served as a military stronghold before becoming a jail. Its advantageous location on a hill afforded a wonderful view of the city and surroundings.

How to get there: The stronghold is located on the northern slopes of Thessaloniki and is accessible by bus, cab, or a reasonable walk from the city center.

What to Do:

Explore the Fortress: Wander among the towers and walls while admiring the views of Thessaloniki.

Learn history: Informational inscriptions and guided tours provide historical context.

Prices:

Admission costs approximately €4 for adults.
Opening hours are typically from 8:00 a.m. to 3:00 p.m. daily.

Fun Factor: The Eptapyrgio Fortress combines historical interest with breathtaking scenery. It's an excellent location for discovering medieval architecture and seeing the cityscape.

5. Philip II's Tomb Overview: The Tomb of Philip II, at Vergina near Thessaloniki, is the final burial place of Alexander the Great's father. The tomb is part of a larger necropolis and is notable for its archeological discoveries.

History: The tomb was discovered in 1977 and dates back to the fourth century BC. It contains priceless artifacts such as gold jewelry and firearms. It contains information about Macedonian royal burial traditions.

How to Get There: The place is approximately 1.5 hours by car from Thessaloniki and may be reached by car or bus. Guided tours are provided for a more in-depth experience.
What to Do:

Explore the Tomb: Investigate the tomb and its contents, especially the beautiful burial objects.
Learn the history: Take a guided tour to better understand the tomb's significance and relics.

Prices:

Admission Fee: Approximately €8 for adults.
Opening hours are typically from 8:00 a.m. to 3:00 p.m. daily.

Fun Factor: The tomb of Philip II is a must-see for historians. The relics and historical background offer an intriguing look at ancient Macedonian monarchy.

6. Roman Baths

The Roman Baths in Thessaloniki highlight the city's historical bathing culture. The site contains well-preserved structures depicting ancient Roman bathing habits.

The baths, which date back to the Roman period, were an important component of ancient Thessaloniki social life. They have complicated heating systems and large bathing rooms.

How to get there: The Roman Baths, located near the city center, are easily accessible by foot or public transportation.

What to Do:

Explore the Structures: Walk around the bathhouse's ruins, including the frigidarium (cold chamber) and caldarium (hot room).

Learn about Roman bathing culture. Informational panels explain why bathing is important in Roman life.

Prices:

Admission costs approximately €6 for adults.

Opening hours are typically from 8:00 a.m. to 3:00 p.m. daily.

Fun Factor: The Roman Baths provide an intriguing glimpse into ancient daily life. The well-preserved remains offer a tangible link to the city's history.

7. Byzantine Bath Overview: The Byzantine Bathhouse, also known as the Vlatadon Monastery Baths, offers insights into Byzantine bathing traditions and design. The site contains the remnants of an ancient bathhouse complex.

History: Built in the fifth century, the Byzantine Bathhouse was part of a larger monastery complex. It emphasizes the importance of community bathing and architectural innovation during the Byzantine period.

How to Get There: The bathhouse is located near the Vlatadon Monastery and may be reached by bus, taxi, or walking from the city center.

What to Do:

Examine the bathhouse's ruins, including the heating systems and bath rooms.

Discover Byzantine Bathing Practices: Informational panels provide background on Byzantine bathing habits and architecture.

Prices:

Admission costs approximately €4 for adults.
Opening hours are typically from 8:00 a.m. to 3:00 p.m. daily.

Fun Factor: The Byzantine Bathhouse provides a unique viewpoint on historical bathing traditions. Its well-preserved structures offer a fascinating look into Byzantine life.

Modern Landmarks

1. Thessaloniki Museum of Photography

Overview:
Part of the MOMUS—Metropolitan Organization of Museums of Visual Arts of Thessaloniki—the Thessaloniki Museum of Photography is a vibrant contemporary museum dedicated to the art of photography. It showcases a diverse range of exhibitions, featuring both Greek and international artists, and acts as a cultural hub for photography enthusiasts.

History:
Founded in 1998, the museum aims to promote and preserve photographic art in Greece. It has since become a prominent venue for historical and contemporary works, hosting regular temporary exhibitions and cultural events, including the annual Thessaloniki Photo Biennale.

How to get there:
The museum is located in Thessaloniki's cultural district, by the waterfront. It is accessible by public transport, including

buses, or a short walk from other city attractions, such as Aristotelous Square.

What to Do:

- **Exhibitions:** View rotating exhibitions that feature both historical and modern photography.
- **Attend Events:** Participate in photography workshops, lectures, and the annual PhotoBiennale.
- **Visit the Bookshop:** Purchase photography books and memorabilia.

Prices:
Admission Fee: Around €5 for adults, with reduced rates for students, seniors, and groups. Special exhibitions may have different pricing.

Opening Hours:
Typically open from 10:00 AM to 6:00 PM, closed on Mondays.

Fun Factor:
The museum offers a dynamic experience for photography lovers, with its engaging exhibitions and educational programs making it a must-visit for visual arts enthusiasts.

2. Thessaloniki International Fair (TIF)

Overview:

The Thessaloniki International Fair (TIF) is a major annual trade event that brings together industries ranging from technology and manufacturing to consumer goods and entertainment. It is one of Greece's most important economic and cultural events, attracting participants from around the world.

History:

Since its inception in 1926, TIF has grown into a key platform for showcasing new technologies, products, and trends, as well as for fostering international business partnerships.

How to get there:

The fairgrounds are located near the city center, accessible via public transport and taxis, and a short walk from the White Tower area.

What to Do:

- **Explore Exhibitions:** Browse through cutting-edge industry exhibits and discover new products and services.
- **Attend seminars and panels:** Engage in discussions on innovation, business, and sustainability.
- **Network:** Connect with professionals and experts in various industries.

Prices:
Admission Fee: Approximately €10 for a day pass, though prices may vary based on specific events and discounts.

Opening Hours:
The fair typically takes place in September and lasts several days, with daily opening hours generally from 10:00 a.m. to 8:00 p.m.

Fun Factor:
TIF provides an exciting atmosphere where you can explore the latest trends across multiple industries. The fair is known for its vibrant mix of exhibitions, technology showcases, and cultural events.

3. Macedonia Palace Hotel

Overview:
A luxurious hotel located on Thessaloniki's waterfront, Macedonia Palace Hotel offers elegant accommodations, panoramic sea views, and high-end amenities. The hotel is a favorite among international travelers and locals alike, blending modern comfort with classic sophistication.

History:
First opened in 1972, the hotel has undergone several renovations to maintain its standing as a premier destination. Over the years, it has hosted dignitaries, celebrities, and

business leaders, remaining an iconic part of Thessaloniki's skyline.

How to get there:
Located along the city's waterfront, the hotel is easily reachable by taxi, private vehicle, or public transport.

What to Do:

- **Enjoy the Views:** Take in sweeping views of the Thermaic Gulf from the hotel's terrace or your room.
- **Dine at the Restaurant:** Indulge in Mediterranean cuisine at the hotel's renowned restaurant, which emphasizes local ingredients.
- **Spa and Wellness:** Unwind at the luxurious spa with a range of treatments and services.

Prices:
Room Rates: Typically range from €150 to €350 per night, depending on the season and room type.
Dining: Meals at the restaurant typically range from €30 to €70 per person.

Fun Factor:
With its prime location, stunning views, and elegant design, Macedonia Palace Hotel provides a truly luxurious retreat for those seeking comfort and sophistication during their stay in Thessaloniki.

4. Thessaloniki Science Center and Technology Museum (NOESIS)

Overview:
NOESIS is a leading science and technology museum in Greece, offering interactive exhibits, a planetarium, and educational programs. It is designed to inspire curiosity in science and technology for visitors of all ages.

History:
Established in 2001, the museum aims to promote science and technology education through hands-on learning and state-of-the-art facilities.

How to get there:
Situated in the northeast of Thessaloniki, NOESIS is accessible by car, bus, or taxi. It's about a 15-minute drive from the city center, with ample parking available.

What to Do:

- **Interactive Exhibits:** Engage with interactive displays covering everything from robotics to astronomy.
- **Planetarium Shows:** Experience immersive shows on space exploration and other scientific topics.
- Join educational workshops for children and adults.

Prices:
Admission Fee: Around €8 for adults, with discounts for children, students, and groups.

Opening Hours:
Generally open from 9:00 AM to 3:00 PM on weekdays and 10:00 AM to 6:00 PM on weekends.

Fun Factor:
NOESIS offers a fascinating and fun way to explore science with its interactive exhibits and state-of-the-art planetarium, making it a top destination for families and science enthusiasts.

5. Valaoritou Area

Overview:
Valaoritou is one of Thessaloniki's trendiest neighborhoods, known for its vibrant nightlife, modern cafes, and live music venues. It's a hotspot for the younger crowd and those seeking to experience the city's modern culture.

History:
Originally a more traditional district, Valaoritou has transformed over the past few decades into a hub for creative expression, contemporary art, and nightlife.

How to get there:
Located centrally, the area is a 10-minute walk from Aristotelous Square and can easily be reached by public transport or taxi.

What to Do:

- **Café Hopping:** Enjoy coffee or drinks in one of the district's many stylish cafes.
- **Nightlife:** Explore the bustling nightlife scene with live music venues, bars, and nightclubs.
- **Cultural Events:** Look out for pop-up galleries, performances, and other cultural events.

Prices:
Cafes: Coffee and drinks generally range from €4 to €10.
Bars: Cocktails and drinks range from €6 to €15.

Fun Factor:
Valaoritou offers a lively and youthful atmosphere, making it an ideal spot for anyone looking to experience Thessaloniki's dynamic contemporary culture.

6. Modiano and Kapani Markets

Overview:
Modiano and Kapani are two of Thessaloniki's most famous markets, offering fresh produce, local delicacies, and

traditional goods. The markets provide a bustling atmosphere where you can experience the city's local culture.

History:
Kapani Market is one of the oldest in Thessaloniki, while Modiano, built in the early 20th century, recently underwent renovations, combining its historic charm with modern updates.

How to get there:
Both markets are located in the heart of the city, a short walk from Aristotelous Square. Public transport options are available, and the markets are accessible on foot.

What to Do:

- **Shop for Fresh Produce:** Purchase fruits, vegetables, and local meats and cheeses.
- **Sample Traditional Foods:** Try local snacks and specialties like koulouri and olives.
- **Explore the Market Stalls:** Wander through the various shops and stalls, where you can buy everything from spices to local wines.

Prices:
Produce and food items typically range from €2 to €10, depending on the products.

Fun Factor:
The vibrant, sensory-rich atmosphere of Modiano and Kapani Markets offers a true taste of local life, making it an essential stop for food lovers and culture enthusiasts.

7. Thessaloniki City Hall

Overview:
Thessaloniki City Hall is a modern architectural landmark that serves as the city's administrative center. It also hosts various public events, exhibitions, and cultural activities throughout the year.

History:
Completed in 1995, the building reflects contemporary architectural trends and serves as an important venue for civic and cultural events.

How to get there:
The City Hall is located near the city center and is easily accessible by foot or public transport.

What to Do:

- **Attend Events:** Check out the schedule for exhibitions, public meetings, and cultural events.
- **Admire the architecture:** look at the building's sleek design and modern features.

Prices:
Admission fee: free for public exhibitions and events.

Opening Hours:
Open during regular business hours, with specific timings for events and exhibitions.

Fun Factor:
Visiting Thessaloniki City Hall provides a glimpse into the city's contemporary urban design and offers opportunities to engage in local cultural activities.

9. Thessaloniki Marina

Overview:
Thessaloniki Marina is a modern marina that provides berths for yachts and leisure boats, as well as restaurants and cafes along the waterfront. It's a scenic spot for dining, walking, or simply enjoying the sea breeze.

History:
In recent years, the marina has become an increasingly popular area for dining and recreation, catering to both locals and tourists.

How to get there:
The marina is located in the Kalamaria district, about a

15-minute drive from the city center. Public transport and taxis are readily available.

What to Do:

- **Dine by the Water:** Enjoy a meal or drink at one of the many waterfront restaurants and cafes.
- **Walk Along the Waterfront:** Take a leisurely stroll and enjoy the view of the boats and the sea.
- **Boat Tours:** Look into boat tours that depart from the marina for a scenic trip along the coastline.

Prices:
Meals at restaurants generally range from €15 to €40 per person.

Fun Factor:
The Thessaloniki Marina offers a peaceful yet lively setting to unwind, with stunning views of the sea and a variety of dining options, making it a great spot for a relaxing day out.

10. Thessaloniki Waterfront Project

Overview:
Thessaloniki Waterfront is an expansive promenade that runs along the city's seafront. It is one of Thessaloniki's most popular public spaces, offering parks, walking paths, art installations, and spectacular views of the Thermaic Gulf.

History:
The revitalization project began in the early 2000s, transforming the waterfront into a vibrant space for leisure and cultural activities. The newest phase includes modern parks and outdoor public art.

How to get there:
The waterfront runs from the White Tower to the Thessaloniki Concert Hall. It's easily accessible on foot, by bike, or via public transport.

What to Do:

- **Stroll the Promenade:** Take a scenic walk along the 5-kilometer promenade.
- **Relax in the Parks:** Visit the themed parks scattered along the waterfront, including the Mediterranean Garden and the Seasons Garden.
- **Public Art:** Explore various outdoor art installations and sculptures.

Prices:
Free to visit, though cafes and restaurants along the way offer refreshments and meals for €10 to €30 per person.

Fun Factor:
The Thessaloniki Waterfront is ideal for leisurely strolls, outdoor activities, and appreciating the city's blend of urban

and natural beauty. It's a great place to relax, whether you're visiting solo or with family.

Scenic Views

1. Mount Hortiatis: Located southeast of Thessaloniki, Mount Hortiatis is a towering natural landmark with panoramic views of the city and Thermaic Gulf. It's a popular hiking and outdoor recreation location that mixes natural beauty with tranquil routes.

Mount Hortiatis, located at an altitude of 1,200 meters, has been a prominent natural feature in Thessaloniki for generations. Its strategic location influenced historical events, and the mountain is home to various flora and wildlife, making it a popular destination for nature enthusiasts.

How to get there:

By car: A 30-minute journey from Thessaloniki takes you to the base of Mount Hortiatis, where parking is provided.
Public transportation: buses connect Thessaloniki with the nearby community of Hortiatis, from which several trails climb up the mountain.

What to Do:

Hiking: Choose from a variety of hiking trails, ranging from beginner-friendly paths to more difficult routes, such as the climb to the top, which provides breathtaking panoramic views.

Picnicking: Scenic locations near the mountain's base are ideal for a quiet picnic in the great outdoors.

Wildlife Watching: The mountain is teeming with wildlife, including a variety of bird species and small mammals.

Prices:

Access is free.

Guided tours are available for approximately €30-€50 per person.

Mount Hortiatis combines natural beauty and physical exertion with spectacular views from the peak, making it a must-see destination for outdoor adventurers.

2. Anopoli (Old Town)

Ano Poli, Thessaloniki's Old Town, boasts classic buildings, small winding lanes, and stunning city vistas. It is a well-preserved region filled with Byzantine and Ottoman-era structures.

History: Ano Poli, one of the few localities that survived the 1917 fire, has preserved its historic character with buildings from the Byzantine and Ottoman periods. It is a living witness to Thessaloniki's rich cultural legacy.

How to get there:

By foot: Walk up from the city center, particularly Egnatia Street.

Public Transportation: Near the Ano Poli gates, buses and taxis can drop you off.

What to Do:

Explore the Streets: Walk around the cobblestone streets, appreciating the classic homes, modest stores, and historic churches.

Visit Viewpoints: Major attractions, such as the Tower of Trigonion, provide breathtaking views of Thessaloniki and the Thermaic Gulf.

Dine Locally: Enjoy traditional Greek cuisine at local tavernas while taking in the neighborhood's unique atmosphere.

Prices:

Access is free.

Dining: Meals at local tavernas run from €10 to €25 per person.

Ano Poli is a historical treasure trove with gorgeous views.

and lovely streets. It's ideal for history aficionados, photographers, and those interested in the city's rich past.

3. White Tower observation platform: The White Tower, Thessaloniki's distinctive landmark, provides a 360-degree observation platform with stunning views of the city and sea.

The White Tower was built in the 15th century and has operated as a fortress and prison. Today, it houses a museum about Thessaloniki's history and culture.

How to get there:

By foot: The White Tower, located along the waterfront, is a short walk from the city center.
Public transportation: buses and taxis can drop you off nearby.
What to Do:

Climb the Tower: Ascend the spiral staircase to the viewing platform, which offers panoramic views over Thessaloniki and the Thermaic Gulf.
Explore the museum: Discover displays that trace the city's history from ancient times to the present.

Prices: Admission costs approximately €6 for adults.
Opening hours are normally from 8:00 a.m. to 8:00 p.m.
The White Tower is a must-see for visitors to Thessaloniki due to its historical significance and breathtaking vistas.

4. Heptapyrgion Fortress

Located on a hill overlooking Thessaloniki, Heptapyrgion Fortress, commonly known as the Seven Towers, dates back to the Byzantine era. It provides panoramic views of the city and the Aegean Sea.

History: The stronghold, built in the 12th century, served as a defensive and penal facility. Today, it serves as a reminder of Thessaloniki's medieval past and sheds light on the city's historical significance.

How to get there:

By foot: Walk up from the city center or Ano Poli.
Public transportation: buses and taxis allow easy access to the fortress entrance.
What to Do:

Explore the Fortress: Wander among the old ruins and see the historical architecture.
Enjoy the Views: The fortress walls offer expansive views over Thessaloniki and its surroundings.
Photography: The fortress is a fantastic location for architectural and panoramic photography.

Prices: Admission is approximately €2 for adults.
Opening hours: 8:00 a.m. to 3:30 p.m.
Heptapyrgion Fortress offers historical interest and breathtaking views, making it ideal for both history and photography enthusiasts.

5. Vardar Riverbank Overview: The Vardar Riverbank, located beside the Axios River, provides a tranquil backdrop with strolling pathways and green spaces. It's an excellent place to unwind and enjoy the picturesque riverbank setting.

The Vardar River, sometimes known as Axios, has played a significant role in regional history. The riverfront has been renovated to give extra recreational area, making it a popular destination for both locals and visitors seeking a calm respite.

How to get there

By foot: The riverbank is accessible from several locations in Thessaloniki's city center.
Public transportation: buses and taxis can take you close to the riverfront area.
What to Do:

Take a leisurely walk or bike ride along the riverbank walkways.

Relax in Green Spaces: Choose a location in the riverside parks to rest and enjoy the natural beauty.

Explore Local Cafes: Take a break at a neighboring café for a drink or food while admiring the sights.

Prices: Access is free.

Dining: Café rates range from €3 to €10.

The Vardar Riverbank offers a serene environment for relaxation and outdoor recreation. Its tranquil surroundings and green areas make it an ideal escape from the hustle and bustle of city life.

6. Kalamaria District Overview: Kalamaria is a picturesque coastal district in Thessaloniki, with breathtaking views of the Thermaic Gulf and calm seaside promenades. It's an ideal location for a relaxing day by the water.

Kalamaria has evolved from a modest fishing village to a lively area with modern amenities, as well as cultural and seaside charm. The lovely promenade is popular with both locals and tourists.

How to get there:

By car: Drive southeast from the city center; ample parking is available in the district.

Kalamaria is easily accessible via public transportation.

including buses and taxis.

What to Do:

Walk the Promenade: Take a leisurely stroll along the picturesque beachfront promenade, taking in the views of the Gulf.

Dine by the Sea: Choose from a variety of seafood restaurants that offer fresh local cuisine while also providing breathtaking sea views.

Visit local stores: Get a flavor of local culture by exploring the district's boutique stores and marketplaces.

Dining: Restaurant costs range from €15 to €35 per person.

Shopping: Prices vary per store.

Kalamaria is a quiet region where visitors may enjoy the ocean, eat fresh seafood, and learn about local culture. It's the perfect setting for a relaxed day by the shore.

7. Mediterranean Cosmos Shopping Center Rooftop

Overview: The Mediterranean Cosmos Shopping Center has a rooftop with magnificent views of Thessaloniki and the surrounding area. It's an excellent place to chill after shopping.

Mediterranean Cosmos, which opened in 2005, is one of the major shopping centers in Thessaloniki. Its rooftop terrace offers a unique vantage point for viewing the cityscape and beyond.

How to get there:

By Car: The shopping center is located on the outskirts of Thessaloniki and has plenty of parking.
Public transportation: buses and taxis can take you right to the shopping center.

What to Do:

Enjoy the Views: Relax on the rooftop and take in the breathtaking views of the city and surroundings.

Shop and Dine: Discover a variety of retailers and restaurants at the shopping complex.

Rooftop Relaxation: Find a space on the rooftop to unwind and breathe fresh air. When you enter the shopping center, you have free access.

Dining: Restaurant prices range from €10 to €30 per person.

The Mediterranean Cosmos rooftop offers a unique view of Thessaloniki's skyline, perfect for a peaceful respite after shopping.

8. Nea Paralia Promenade Overview: Thessaloniki's waterfront area has been nicely rebuilt. It's ideal for beautiful hikes, with tranquil views of the sea and city.

Nea Paralia is part of Thessaloniki's new waterfront makeover, aiming to provide more public places for both citizens and tourists. The neighborhood is now one of the city's most popular sites for recreational activities.

How to get there:

Walking is an easy way to get from the city center.
By public transportation: buses and taxis may transport you to various locations along the promenade.

What to Do:

Stroll the Promenade: Enjoy a leisurely walk along the waterfront, which offers spectacular views of the sea and modern architecture.
Relax in Public Spaces: The promenade is lined with well-kept parks and green spaces, perfect for unwinding.
Visit surrounding attractions: Spend the day exploring nearby sights and restaurants.
Prices: Access is free.
Dining: Prices at surrounding restaurants range from €15 to €40 per person.
The Nea Paralia Promenade offers a tranquil promenade along the lake, making it a fun destination for visitors. It's a popular spot for both locals and visitors to relax and enjoy the beauty of Thessaloniki's shoreline.

Churches and Monasteries

1. Saint Demetrius Church (Agios Dimitrios).
The Church of Saint Demetrius is the largest and most prominent religious site in Thessaloniki, devoted to the city's

patron saint. The basilica dates from the fourth century AD, but it has been restored multiple times owing to fires and devastation.

History: Originally built under Emperor Galerius in the fourth century, the modern five-aisled basilica was rebuilt after a fire in the seventh century. The church was also used as a mosque during Ottoman occupation before being restored back into a church in 1912 after Thessaloniki was liberated. It was further renovated after the 1917 fire.

What to Do: Visitors can tour the restored Byzantine mosaics and the crypt, which houses Saint Demetrius' relics and items recovered from past fires.

Admission is free; however, donations are encouraged.
The church celebrates Saint Demetrius' feast day on October 26th, which coincides with Thessaloniki's freedom day.

2. Saint George's Church (Agios Georgios)—Rounda

This large circular monument, commonly known as the Rotunda, was originally a Roman mausoleum before becoming a Christian church. Its massive dimensions and spectacular internal mosaics make it an intriguing historical landmark.

History: Originally built by Emperor Galerius in the early fourth century, it was later converted into a Christian church.

under Emperor Theodosius I. During the Ottoman period, it was used as a mosque before being reconverted in 1912.

What to Do: Admire the stunning mosaics that cover the dome and walls. These mosaics are among the world's oldest Christian art items.
Prices: Entry fees apply, which normally range from €2 to €5.
Fun fact: The Rotunda is one of Thessaloniki's earliest Christian churches.

3. Church of St. Sophia (Agia Sophia)
This Byzantine church, inspired by the Hagia Sophia in Constantinople, is a stunning example of early Christian architecture, complete with spectacular mosaics and a fascinating history.

History: The church was established in the eighth century and operated as a cathedral before becoming a mosque under Ottoman authority. It was transformed into a church in the early twentieth century.

What to Do: Visitors can examine the exquisite mosaics representing religious motifs. The central dome, in particular, provides breathtaking vistas of Christ Pantocrator.
Prices: Admission is free; however, donations are welcome.
The church in Thessaloniki, a key Byzantine hub, combines early Christian and Byzantine architectural styles.

4. The monastery of Vlatadon.

This 14th-century monastery, located on the heights of Ano Poli, is a tranquil location with panoramic views of the city. It is still an active religious site, as well as one of Thessaloniki's UNESCO-listed structures.

The monastery was founded by the monks Dorotheos and Markos Vlates, Gregory Palamas' pupils. It was an important center for Orthodox monastic life and learning.

What to Do: Visit the modest museum, which displays religious documents and artifacts, and stroll around the tranquil grounds.

Prices: Entry is usually free, but donations are accepted.

The monastery, known for its theological studies, offers stunning panoramic views of Thessaloniki and is renowned for its theological studies.

5. Church of Panagia Chalkeon.

This 11th-century Byzantine church, located in the city center, is well preserved and known for its stunning murals and eye-catching architecture.

History: Christophoros, a royal officer, built the church in 1028 as a family church. The name is derived from the adjacent metalworkers' neighborhood (Chalkeon = copper in Greek).

What to Do: Visitors can view the beautiful frescoes and learn about their historical significance during the Byzantine period.
Prices: Entry is free.
The church's interior frescoes are a prime example of 11th-century Byzantine art (Greekacom).

CHAPTER SIX
Food and Drink in Thessaloniki

Thessaloniki is a gastronomic delight, blending Greek tradition with modern influences. Here's a guide to the **must-try foods and drinks in Thessaloniki**, including traditional dishes, popular street food, and where you can find them.

1. Bougatsa (Μπουγάτσα)

What it is: a flaky pastry typically filled with semolina custard (sweet version) or minced meat and cheese (savory version). For the sweet variety, we serve it warm and dust it with powdered sugar or cinnamon.

Ingredients: phyllo dough, semolina custard (or minced meat and cheese for savory), powdered sugar, and cinnamon.

Estimated price: €1.50-€3 per portion.

Where to try:

- **Bougatsa Giannis** (Pavlou Mela 22)—a popular spot for traditional bougatsa.
- **Serraikon Bougatsa (Vasileos Irakleiou 8) is one of the city's oldest and most cherished shops.**

2. Souvlaki (Σουβλάκι)

What it is: skewered grilled meat, often served with pita bread, tomatoes, onions, tzatziki, and fries. A classic street food found throughout Greece.

Ingredients: pork or chicken, pita bread, tomatoes, onions, tzatziki, olive oil, and spices.

Price estimate: €2.50-€4 per souvlaki.

Where to try:

- **O Kostas** (Mitropoleos 100) is known for its succulent souvlaki.
- **Derlicatessen** (Karaoli & Dimitriou 8) offers both traditional and modern twists on souvlaki.

3. Gyro (Γύρος)

What it is: A close cousin of souvlaki, gyro consists of meat (usually pork or chicken) cooked on a vertical rotisserie, sliced thin, and served in pita bread with various toppings like tzatziki, tomatoes, onions, and fries.

Ingredients: pork or chicken, pita bread, tomatoes, onions, fries, tzatziki, olive oil, and spices.

Estimated price: €2.50-€4.50 per gyro.

Where to try:

- **Gyros Aristotelous** (Aristotelous Square)—a local favorite.
- **Savouras** (Egnatia 124) is famous for its delicious gyros.

4. Koulouri Thessalonikis (Κουλούρι Θεσσαλονίκης)

What it is: a circular bread ring covered in sesame seeds, often sold by street vendors early in the morning. It's soft inside with a crispy crust.

Ingredients: flour, water, yeast, sesame seeds, and olive oil.

Price Estimate: Around €0.50-€1 per piece.

Where to try: Street vendors all over the city, especially around **Aristotelous Square** and **Egnatia Street**.

5. Patsa (Πατσάς)

What it is: A traditional soup made from tripe (intestines), often served as a late-night meal. It's believed to be a great hangover cure.

Ingredients: beef or pork tripe, garlic, vinegar, and broth.

Estimated price: €5-€7 per portion.

Where to try:

- **Diagonios** (Psaropoula area)—one of the best-known places for traditional pasta.

6. Soutzoukakia Smyrneika (Σουτζουκάκια Σμυρνέικα)

What it is: A dish from Smyrna consisting of spiced meatballs cooked in a rich tomato sauce, typically served with rice or mashed potatoes.

Ingredients: minced beef or pork, garlic, cumin, onions, tomatoes, olive oil, and spices.

Estimated price: €7-€10 per portion.

Where to try:

- **To Elliniko** (Mitropoleos 54)—a great spot for traditional dishes, including soutzoukakia.

7. Tiganites Patates (Τηγανιτές Πατάτες)

What it is: Simple yet addictive, these are fried potatoes (Greek-style fries), often served as a side dish to many dishes.

Ingredients: potatoes, olive oil, oregano, and salt.

Price Estimate: €2-€4 per serving.

Where to try: Available in almost every taverna and street food joint, but highly recommended at **Halaro Tavern** (Mitropoleos Street).

8. Tsoureki (Τσουρέκι)

What it is: sweet, braided bread with a soft, fluffy texture. It is sometimes stuffed with chocolate or chestnuts and flavored with mahleb (a unique spice).

Ingredients: flour, sugar, butter, eggs, mahleb, and sometimes fillings like chocolate or chestnut.

Price estimate: €3-€7, depending on size and fillings.

Where to try:

- **Terkenlis** (Tsimiski Street) is a famous bakery known for its legendary tsoureki with various fillings.

9. Ouzo (Ούζο)

What it is: a popular Greek aperitif flavored with anise. It's often enjoyed with meze (small appetizers like olives and cheese).

Ingredients: alcohol, anise, water.

Price Estimate: €3-€5 for a glass at a taverna.

Where to try: Almost any taverna will serve ouzo, but for a fantastic experience, try it at **Rouga Tavern** (Karipi 28).

10. Frappe (Φραπέ)

What it is: a cold, frothy coffee drink made from instant coffee, water, and sugar. It's a beloved drink, especially during the summer.

Ingredients: instant coffee, water, sugar, milk (optional), ice cubes.

Price estimate: €2-€3.50 per drink.

Where to try: Any café in Thessaloniki, but **Ergon Agora** (Pindou 1) provides a great setting to enjoy one.

11. Moussaka (Μουσακάς)

What it is: One of Greece's most famous dishes, moussaka is a rich and hearty casserole made of layers of eggplant, ground meat (usually beef or lamb), and a creamy béchamel sauce on top. It's baked until golden and served as a main course.

Ingredients: eggplants, potatoes, ground meat (beef or lamb), tomatoes, onions, garlic, bechamel sauce, cheese, olive oil.

Estimated price: €8-€12 per portion.

Where to try:

- **Ouzou Melathron** (Karipi 21)—a traditional taverna known for its excellent moussaka.
- **To Koutouki Tou Antoni** (Paparrigopoulou 8)—a cozy spot offering a homemade version of the dish.

12. Dolmades (Ντολμαδάκια)

What it is: Grape leaves stuffed with rice, herbs, and occasionally ground meat, dolmades are served as an appetizer or a main dish. They are commonly enjoyed with a drizzle of lemon juice or yogurt on the side.

Ingredients: vinegar leaves, rice, ground meat (optional), onions, dill, mint, lemon, olive oil.

Estimated price: €5-€7 per portion.

Where to try:

- **Kritikos Gallery & Restaurants** (Ionos Dragoumi 5) is famous for its authentic dolmades.
- **Taverna Igglis** (Eptapyrgiou 115) is a family-run place with a reputation for traditional dishes.

13. Pastitsio (Παστίτσιο)

What it is: a Greek baked pasta dish, similar to lasagna, with layers of pasta, ground meat, and béchamel sauce. It's a favorite comfort food across Greece.

Ingredients: Pasta (usually bucatini), ground meat (beef or lamb), béchamel sauce, tomatoes, cheese, eggs, butter, olive oil, spices.

Estimated price: €7-€10 per portion.

Where to try:

- **Mpougatsa Peloponnisou (Nik. Plastira 52) is well-known for its homemade pastries.**
- **Ta Varelia** (Filippou 36) is a small taverna known for its traditional pastitsio.

14. Seafood Meze (Θαλασσινά Μεζέ)

What it is: Thessaloniki's proximity to the sea means an abundance of fresh seafood. Meze is a selection of small dishes, perfect for sharing. Expect octopus, fried calamari, shrimp saganaki (shrimp in a tomato-based sauce with feta cheese), grilled sardines, and mussels.

Ingredients: Octopus, squid, shrimp, mussels, tomatoes, feta cheese, lemon, olive oil, oregano.

Price estimate: €6-€15, depending on the seafood and portion size.

Where to try:

- **7 Thalasses** (Kalapothaki 10) is a high-end restaurant with excellent seafood menu options.
- **Mpakaliarakia tou Aristou** (Ionos Dragoumi 39) is great for seafood lovers, especially their fried calamari.

15. Biftekia (Μπιφτέκια)

What it is: Greek-style meat patties, usually made with ground beef or a mixture of beef and pork, seasoned with herbs and spices. They are grilled and served with fries or salad. It's a flavorful and satisfying dish.

Ingredients: ground beef or pork, breadcrumbs, onions, garlic, oregano, mint, olive oil, and lemon.

Estimated price: €8-€12 per portion.

Where to try:

- **Zythos Dore** (Mitropoleos 50) is a traditional Greek restaurant known for its biftekia.
- **Exostrefis Taverna** (K. Paleologou 3) offers perfectly grilled biftekia.

16. Saganaki (Σαγανάκι)

What it is: A fried cheese dish, saganaki is made by pan-searing cheese (usually graviera, kefalotyri, or feta) until golden and crispy. It's a popular meze served with a squeeze of lemon.

Ingredients: graviera or kefalotyri cheese, flour, olive oil, lemon.

Estimated price: €4-€6 per portion.

Where to try:

- **Mpakalogatos** (Olympiou Diamanti 5): a well-loved taverna for saganaki.
- **Kafenio tou Yannis** (Valaoritou 10)—another great spot for traditional Greek appetizers.

17. Skepasti (Σκεπαστή)

What it is: Skepasti is like a Greek "sandwich" made with two layers of pita bread, often stuffed with grilled meat, cheese, tomatoes, and fries. It's usually served in large portions, perfect for sharing.

Ingredients: pita bread, pork or chicken, cheese, tomatoes, fries, tzatziki.

Estimated price: €6-€9 per portion.

Where to try:

- **Kafeneio Elliniko** (Mitropoleos 45) is known for its skepasti with juicy meat.
- **Tzaki Hozi** (Egnatia 96) is famous for its hearty skepasti.

18. Revani (Ρεβανί)

What it is: A traditional semolina cake soaked in syrup, often flavored with orange or lemon. It's a sweet treat usually served at the end of a meal.

Ingredients: semolina, eggs, sugar, butter, syrup (sugar, water, lemon/orange zest).

Estimated price: €3-€5 per portion.

Where to try:

- **Elia Lemoni** (Sofouli 38)—a charming spot known for its delicious revani.
- **Trigona Elenidis** (Delfon 86) is also famous for its other Greek desserts.

19. Trigona Panoramatos (Τρίγωνα Πανοράματος)

What it is: A popular dessert in Thessaloniki, these triangle-shaped phyllo pastries are filled with custard cream and sometimes topped with syrup. It's a must-try for any visitor with a sweet tooth.

Ingredients: phyllo dough, custard cream, syrup, sugar, butter.

Price estimate: €2-€4 per piece.

Where to try:

- **Trigona Elenidis** (Panorama area) is the most famous place for this dessert.
- **Sergiani Pastry Shop** (Kassandrou Street)—another great bakery for authentic trigona.

20. Baklava (Μπακλαβάς)

What it is: a rich, sweet pastry made of layers of phyllo dough filled with chopped nuts and sweetened with syrup or honey. It's one of the most iconic desserts in Greece.

Ingredients: phyllo dough, walnuts or pistachios, honey or syrup, butter.

Estimated price: €3-€5 per portion.

Where to try:

- **Hatzifotiou** (Proxenou Koromila 36) is known for its excellent Baklava.
- **Blé Vin** (Tsimiski 60) is a modern pastry shop with top-notch Greek desserts.

21. Tzatziki (Τζατζίκι)

What it is: a classic Greek dip made from yogurt, cucumber, garlic, and olive oil. It's served as an appetizer or a side dish and pairs perfectly with grilled meats, pita bread, or vegetable dishes.

Ingredients: Greek yogurt, cucumbers, garlic, olive oil, vinegar, salt, and dill.

Price Estimate: €3-€5 per serving.

Where to try:

- **Rouga** (Karipi 28) is a lovely taverna where you can try tzatziki as part of a meze platter.

- **Ergon Agora** (Pindou 1): a trendy spot with great food, including traditional tzatziki.

Street Food You Must Try

- **Loukoumades (Λουκουμάδες)**: These are Greek doughnuts, deep-fried and drizzled with honey or chocolate. Available at street vendors in **Modiano Market** or **Kapani Market**.

  - **Price**: €2-€3 per portion.
- **Tiganites (Τηγανίτες)**: Greek pancakes often served with honey or fruits found at street vendors, especially in **Ano Poli** (Upper Town).

  - **Price**: €1.50-€3 per serving.
- **Peinirli (Πεϊνιρλί)**: A boat-shaped dough filled with cheese and other toppings like ham or bacon, often found in local bakeries.

  - **Where to Try**: **Panos Bakery** (Egnatia 30).
  - **Price**: €3-€5 per piece.

Best street food hotspots

- **Modiano Market**: The go-to market for fresh produce, spices, and local street food. You can grab koulouri, loukoumades, or fresh gyros here.
- **Kapani Market**: This is another traditional market where you can experience the essence of local Thessaloniki street food.
- **Ladadika District**: A vibrant area filled with tavernas and street food vendors. This is a must-visit spot to try souvlaki, gyros, and seafood.
- **Aristotelous Square**: The heart of Thessaloniki, where you can find street vendors selling local snacks like koulouri and loukoumades. The area is also packed with cafes and taverns.
- **Ano Poli (Upper Town):** If you want to experience authentic Thessaloniki in a more traditional setting, Ano Poli (Upper Town) is the place to be. Here, you'll find local eateries serving skepasti, peinirli, and grilled meats.

Exploring Thessaloniki's Culinary Delights: A Guide to Must-Try Spots

As you wander the lively streets of Thessaloniki, the blend of aromas from fresh coffee, sizzling souvlaki, and sweet pastries will guide you through the city's rich culinary landscape. Known as Greece's food capital, Thessaloniki offers a mix of traditional flavors and modern twists. This guide takes you through the best places to enjoy great food, coffee, and cocktails, whether you're looking for a casual snack or a sophisticated dining experience.

La Nonna

Location: **Tsimiski Street**

Picture This: Walking down Tsimiski Street, you spot the elegant yet cozy **La Nonna**. The rich smell of Greek coffee and the sight of beautifully arranged pastries pull you in. The outdoor seating is perfect for people-watching while sipping on a classic beer.

What to Try:

- **Greek Coffee**: Traditional and rich, served with a glass of water, perfect for a slow, relaxing coffee break.
- **Homemade Cheesecake**: creamy, indulgent, and just sweet enough to satisfy your dessert cravings.

Vibe: A mix of old-school charm and modern elegance, La Nonna is ideal for a leisurely coffee or dessert while escaping the city's hustle and bustle.

Tip: Take your time and soak in the atmosphere. It's an ideal spot to unwind after a day of exploring.

Prices:

- **Greek coffee**: €3-€5
- **Cheesecake**: €4-€7

How to Get There: Centrally located on **Tsimiski Street**, easily accessible by foot or public transport.

Vogatsikou 3

Location: 3 Vogatsikou Street, Thessaloniki 54622

Picture This: As night falls, you find yourself in **Vogatsikou 3**, a stylish cocktail bar. The dim lighting and chic decor create the perfect atmosphere for an intimate evening. You sink into a plush seat and browse their cocktail list, each drink crafted to be a sensory experience.

What to Try:

- **Signature Cocktails**: Known for their innovative and creative cocktails, with ingredients and combinations that will surprise and delight your palate.

Vibe: Sophisticated and artistic, perfect for those who appreciate refined cocktails in a modern, elegant setting.

Tip: The bartenders are mixologists at heart, so don't hesitate to ask for something off-menu or a personalized recommendation.

Prices:

- **Cocktails**: €8-€12

How to Get There: **3 Vogatsikou Street**, centrally located in a fashionable part of the city.

Bistro La Vie

Location: **Navarinou Street**

Picture This: On a sunny Saturday morning, you walk into **Bistro La Vie**, welcomed by the scent of freshly baked goods and rich coffee. The cozy interior is bustling with a brunch crowd, making it the perfect place to enjoy a laid-back meal.

What to Try:

- **Greek Yogurt with Honey and Fresh Fruit**: A fresh and wholesome breakfast option, ideal for a light start to your day.
- **Freshly Baked Pastries: Their pastries are irresistible—flaky, sweet, and made with love.**

Vibe: cozy, warm, and welcoming—a perfect spot for brunch with friends or a quiet coffee break.

Tip: Their pastries are made fresh daily, so don't hesitate to ask what's just out of the oven!

Prices:

- **Brunch items**: €5-€8
- **Pastries**: €2-€4

How to Get There: Located on **Navarinou Street**, just a short walk from the city center.

Bar-B-Q

Location: **Tsimiski Street**

Picture This: The scent of sizzling meats fills the air as you enter **Bar-B-Q**, a lively, casual spot where the focus is on smoky, flavorful barbecue dishes. The atmosphere is vibrant, making it a perfect choice for a fun evening out with friends.

What to Try:

- **Barbecue Dishes**: Whether it's ribs, grilled chicken, or steak, everything is perfectly seasoned and cooked.
- **House Barbecue Sauce**: Their signature tangy and rich sauce elevates every dish.

Vibe: Lively, laid-back, and perfect for a night out with great food and company.

Tip: Ask for extra sauce—it's a house specialty and pairs beautifully with any barbecue dish.

Prices:

- **Main barbecue dishes: €10-€15**
- **Sides**: €3-€5

How to Get There: Conveniently located on **Tsimiski Street**, making it a central stop for dinner.

Sasa's Bar

Location: **Monastiriou Street**

Picture This: The city lights glimmer as you enter **Sasa's Bar**, a sleek and trendy lounge. The stylish setting and impressive wine list set the tone for an evening of relaxation and enjoyment.

What to Try:

- **Selection of Wines: The wine list is extensive and carefully curated, from local to international labels.**
- **Creative Cocktails**: beautifully crafted cocktails that balance flavor, aroma, and presentation.

Vibe: trendy and stylish, yet relaxed enough to enjoy a low-key evening with friends.

Tip: Ask the bartenders for their wine recommendations—they're experts in pairing wine with your mood or meal.

Prices:

- **Wines**: €5-€10 per glass.
- **Cocktails**: €8-€12

Get there: Monastiriou Street is central and perfect for an evening out.

The Little Big Café

Location: **Agias Sofias Street**

Picture This: You step into **The Little Big Café**, a cozy, quirky spot perfect for an afternoon coffee break. The aroma of freshly brewed coffee fills the air as you settle in with a book or catch up with a friend over delicious homemade pastries.

What to Try:

- **Specialty Coffee**: Freshly brewed with rich flavors that make it the perfect afternoon pick-me-up.
- **Homemade Pastries**: Seasonal and baked fresh daily, the pastries are always a highlight.

Vibe: Quirky, inviting, and perfect for a casual coffee break or a quiet afternoon alone.

Tip: Their pastries change with the seasons, so ask about the specials for a unique treat.

Prices:

- **Coffee**: €3-€5
- **Pastries**: €2-€4

How to Get There: Located on **Agias Sofias Street**, centrally located for a convenient stop during your day.

The Urban Grill

Location: **Tsimiski Street**

Picture This: As you walk into **The Urban Grill**, the energy of the evening is palpable. The smell of gourmet burgers grilling fills the air, and the lively atmosphere invites you in for a fun, hearty meal.

What to Try:

- **Gourmet Burgers**: Juicy patties with unique toppings and flavors that take the humble burger to the next level.
- **Craft Beers**: Their selection of local and international craft beers is the perfect pairing for your meal.

Vibe: Modern and dynamic, ideal for a casual yet satisfying dinner with friends.

Tip: Try pairing your burger with one of their craft beers. The staff is pleased to recommend the perfect pairing.

Prices:

- **Burgers**: €8-€12
- **Craft Beers**: €4-€6

How to Get There: Located on **Tsimiski Street**, simple to reach and ideal for a casual night out.

Extra popular spots to explore in Thessaloniki:

Ergon Agora

Location: **Pindou 1**

- **Vibe**: A trendy marketplace offering artisanal Greek products, including meze dishes and local wines.
- **What to Try**: Traditional Greek meze, craft coffee, and Greek yogurt.
- **Prices**: €5-€15 depending on the menu items.

Elia Lemoni

Location: **Sofouli 38**

- **Vibe**: A traditional Greek taverna with a welcoming, family-friendly atmosphere.
- **What to Try**: **Moussaka**, **Souvlaki**, and **Revani** (a syrup-soaked semolina cake).
- **Prices**: €8-€12 for main dishes.

Trigona Elenidis

Location: **Panorama**

- **Vibe is known for their famous Trigona Panoramatos, a pastry filled with creamy custard.**
- **What to Try**: The signature **Trigona**—a must-have dessert.
- **Prices**: €2-€4 per piece.

Sempriko

Location: Fragkon 2

- **Vibe**: Modern yet cozy, **Sempriko** serves up delicious Greek and Mediterranean fusion dishes.
- **Soutzoukakia (spiced meatballs in tomato sauce) and seafood pasta are two things to try.**
- **Prices**: €12-€20 for main dishes.

To Elliniko

Location: Mitropolos 54

- **Vibe**: A traditional Greek taverna with authentic flavors and a lively atmosphere.
- **What to Try: Soutzoukakia, Greek salad**, and **stuffed vine leaves**.
- **Prices**: €8-€15 per dish.

Estrella

Location: Pavlou Mela 48

- **Vibe**: A lively café known for its famous **bougatsa pancakes** and all-day breakfast options.
- **What to Try: Bougatsa Pancakes** (a modern twist on the classic Greek pastry) and **avocado toast**.
- **Prices**: €6-€10 for breakfast dishes.

Nightclubs in Thessaloniki

La Luna:

- **Description**: **La Luna** is a well-known nightclub offering a mix of Greek and international music. It's the perfect spot for dancing until the early hours, with a lively atmosphere and a great crowd. Expect a mix of both local hits and global dance music.
- **Vibe**: energetic and fun, ideal for dancing enthusiasts.

Remvi:

- **Description**: **Remvi** is a hotspot for both live music and DJ sets. This venue offers a varied musical experience, catering to different tastes, from traditional Greek tunes to more contemporary hits. The venue is known for its great views, lively ambiance, and diverse crowd.
- **Vibe**: A mix of live performances and DJ sets, offering something for everyone.

KooKoo:

- **Description**: **KooKoo** is a centrally located venue, popular for its eclectic mix of music genres, including house, indie, and more. It attracts a diverse crowd of locals and visitors, making it a fun and lively place to spend the night.
- **Vibe**: Modern and vibrant, with an open-minded crowd and a range of music styles.

Vogue Club:

- **Description**: One of the largest and most popular nightclubs in Thessaloniki, **Vogue Club** offers a mix of Greek and international music, attracting a young, energetic crowd. It's known for its lively atmosphere and impressive light shows.

- **Vibe is high-energy, making it ideal for dancing and late-night fun.**

Markiz Club:

- **Description**: **Markiz** is a popular nightclub located near the city center, offering a mix of Greek hits and international music. Known for its packed dance floor and vibrant atmosphere, it's a must-visit for anyone looking to experience Thessaloniki's night scene.
- **Vibe**: Lively and youthful, with a party atmosphere.

Shark Bar-Restaurant:

- **Description**: While more of a high-end bar-restaurant during the day, **Shark** transforms into a vibrant club at night, especially during weekends. With a mix of commercial, house, and R&B music, it attracts a stylish crowd looking for an upscale night out.
- **Vibe**: Upscale and chic, ideal for those who want a more refined nightclub experience.

W Nightclub:

- ○ **Description**: Known for its sleek decor and modern vibe, **W Nightclub** focuses on electronic music and hosts well-known DJs from Greece and abroad. The club has a stylish and luxurious atmosphere, making it a popular spot for those into house and techno.
- ○ **Vibe**: Modern, with an emphasis on electronic music and high-end vibes.

Eightball Club:

- ○ **Description**: A well-known club for rock, punk, and metal lovers. **Eightball** hosts themed nights with live bands and DJs, often blending live music with a club atmosphere. This is the go-to spot for fans of alternative music scenes.
- ○ **Vibe**: edgy and underground, perfect for those who enjoy rock and alternative genres.

Live Music Venues in Thessaloniki

❖ **Principal Club Theater**:

- ➢ **Description**: **Principal Club Theater** is a premier venue for live music in Thessaloniki.

Hosting both local and international artists, this club offers an exceptional atmosphere for concerts, with great acoustics and a spacious layout. The music ranges from rock to electronic and alternative.

  ➢ **Vibe**: One of the city's top destinations for serious music lovers.

❖ **Mylos Complex**:

  ➢ **Description**: **Mylos** is a cultural and entertainment hub that includes several stages and spaces for live music, theater, and exhibitions. It hosts a variety of genres, from jazz and rock to electronic and world music. It's a wonderful spot to enjoy live performances in a vibrant setting.

  ➢ **Vibe**: A mix of cultural and musical events, perfect for those looking for something beyond the typical nightclub experience.

❖ **Salonica**:

  ➢ **Description**: **Salonica** is a smaller, intimate venue that offers regular live performances, often featuring acoustic sets and jazz. It's a cozy spot for those who prefer a relaxed, laid-back atmosphere with quality music.

➤ **Vibe**: intimate and inviting, ideal for enjoying a quiet night with live music.

❖ **Block 33**:

➤ **Description**: **Block 33** is a multipurpose cultural venue that hosts live music events ranging from rock and jazz to electronic and hip-hop. It's a favorite spot for both local and international artists and has a loyal fan base.

➤ **Vibe**: Underground and eclectic, with a diverse lineup of music genres.

❖ **The Residents**:

➤ **Description**: **The Residents** is a small, intimate venue known for its unique jazz and indie music performances. With cozy seating and an inviting atmosphere, it's a wonderful place to enjoy live music in a relaxed setting.

➤ **Vibe**: intimate and cozy, ideal for jazz and indie lovers.

❖ **Gaia Live**:

➤ **Description**: **Gaia Live** is a venue for live performances, hosting everything from jazz to ethnic music. It's particularly known for its high-quality acoustics and welcoming

atmosphere, attracting a loyal audience that appreciates diverse music genres.
  - ➤ **Vibe**: Friendly and welcoming, with a focus on live, world music performances.
- ❖ **WE**:

  - ➤ **Description**: **WE** is a multifunctional venue that not only hosts live music but also cultural events, festivals, and parties. It has become a hub for alternative and underground music scenes, featuring both live bands and DJ sets across a range of genres.
  - ➤ **Vibe**: Alternative and underground, perfect for those who enjoy cutting-edge music and events.

Late-Night Eateries in Thessaloniki

Modiano and Kapani Markets:

  - ➤ **Description**: After a night out, the **Modiano** and **Kapani Markets** are go-to spots for late-night bites. You can find street vendors offering traditional Greek street food like souvlaki, gyros, and other delicious snacks. These markets are also great places to soak up the local atmosphere.

➢ **Vibe**: Bustling and authentic, perfect for grabbing a quick bite on the go.

Late-night Souvlaki Joints:

➢ **Description**: Thessaloniki is full of late-night souvlaki bars, and many of them stay open well into the early morning hours. Whether you're craving a gyro or a souvlaki pita, these street food vendors are scattered throughout the city and are ideal for a quick and delicious snack after a night out.
➢ **Vibe**: Casual and convenient, perfect for satisfying post-club hunger.

Derlicatessen:

➢ **Description**: **Derlicatessen** is a famous late-night spot offering delicious souvlaki, gyros, and other grilled meats. Known for its quick service and tasty food, it's a popular choice for a post-party snack in the early morning hours.
➢ **Vibe**: Casual and perfect for late-night cravings after clubbing.

Brothers in Law:

➢ **Description**: If you're in the mood for gourmet burgers after a night out, **Brothers in Law** is open late and serves some of the best burgers in Thessaloniki. With a variety of toppings and craft beer options, it's a wonderful place to refuel.

➢ **Vibe**: Modern and casual, ideal for a relaxed but tasty late-night meal.

Tsarouchas:

➢ **Description**: For those who want something more substantial after a long night, **Tsarouchas** is a 24/7 restaurant that serves hearty Greek meals, including their famous (tripe soup), which is said to be the ultimate hangover cure.

➢ **Vibe**: Traditional and comforting, ideal for late-night (or early morning) meals.

Ladokolla:

➢ **Description**: **Ladokolla** is a casual grill house known for its late-night service, offering souvlaki, grilled meats, and fries. It's a favorite among locals who want a quick, satisfying meal after a night out.

➢ **Vibe**: Casual and no-frills, perfect for those who want something quick and filling.

Pizza Chris:

> ➤ **Description**: **Pizza Chris** is a local favorite for grabbing a slice of pizza late at night. It's affordable, fast, and the perfect snack to grab on your way home after clubbing.
> ➤ **Vibe**: Laid-back, with quick service and affordable prices.

Additional Tips for Enjoying Thessaloniki's Nightlife

1. **Check local listings**:

   ○ Thessaloniki's nightlife scene is always changing, so it's a beneficial idea to check local event listings or ask locals for recommendations on where to go. Clubs and bars often have special events or themed nights, which can make your night out even more exciting.

2. **Dress Code**:

   ○ While many bars in Thessaloniki have a relaxed, casual atmosphere, some nightclubs, especially upscale venues, may enforce a dress code. It's always a good idea to check ahead of time to ensure you're dressed appropriately.

3. **Public Transport and Taxis**:

   ○ Public transport in Thessaloniki can be limited late at night, so taxis or ride-sharing services like Uber or Beat are reliable options to get home safely after a night out.

CHAPTER SEVEN

Outdoor Adventures and Excursions in Thessaloniki

Thessaloniki isn't just about delicious food and vibrant city life—it's also a gateway to incredible outdoor adventures. Whether you're a nature lover, an adrenaline junkie, or someone who simply enjoys a leisurely stroll, Thessaloniki offers a variety of activities to get you moving and exploring.

From relaxing beach days to thrilling off-road adventures, this guide will help you navigate the best outdoor experiences Thessaloniki has to offer.

1. Beach Days: Sun, Sand, and Sea

Perea Beach

- **What to Expect**: Perea is one of the closest beaches to Thessaloniki, known for its crystal-clear waters and vibrant beach bars. It's a favorite among locals for sunbathing, swimming, and enjoying the summer breeze.
- **Facilities**: You'll find plenty of sunbeds, umbrellas, and beachside cafes where you can grab a snack or drink.
- **Prices**: Renting sunbeds and umbrellas typically costs around €5-€10 per day. Drinks and snacks range from €3-€10 at beach bars.
- **How to get there:** Easily accessible by bus or a short 20-30 minute drive from Thessaloniki.
- **Tip**: Head there early in the morning to secure a favorable spot and enjoy a peaceful swim before the crowds arrive.

Agia Triada Beach

- **What to Expect**: Located near Perea, **Agia Triada** offers a quieter beach experience with fewer tourists. The waters are calm and perfect for swimming.

- **Facilities**: Sunbeds, umbrellas, and beach bars are available, though the vibe is more laid-back compared to Perea.
- **Prices**: Similar to Perea, expect to pay €5-€10 for sunbeds and umbrellas, while food and drinks range from €3-€10.
- **How to Get There**: A 30-minute drive or bus ride from Thessaloniki.
- **Tip**: Perfect for families and those seeking a more relaxed beach day.

2. Water sports: excitement on the waves

Thessaloniki Marina

- **What to Expect**: The marina is a hub for water sports enthusiasts. You can enjoy activities like windsurfing, jet skiing, paddleboarding, and sailing.
- **Facilities**: Several rental shops offer equipment and lessons for all skill levels.
- **Prices**:
    - Windsurfing lessons: €40-€60 per hour.
    - Jet Ski rental: €60-€90 for 30 minutes.
    - Paddleboarding: €20-€30 per hour.
- **How to Get There**: The marina is centrally located, easily reachable by taxi or a short walk from most parts of Thessaloniki.

- **Tip**: Book in advance during summer to secure your spot and avoid long wait times.

Halkidiki Peninsula (Kassandra)

- **What to Expect**: Halkidiki is famous for its pristine beaches and crystal-clear waters, making it ideal for snorkeling, diving, and other water sports. Kassandra, the first leg of Halkidiki, is particularly popular for water sports.
- **Facilities**: Numerous beach resorts and rental shops offer equipment for water sports, including kayaking, scuba diving, and windsurfing.
- **Prices**:
  - Snorkeling equipment rental: Around €20-€30.
  - Kayak rentals: €10-€20 per hour.
  - Scuba diving packages: €60-€100.
- **How to Get There**: Halkidiki is about a 1-hour drive from Thessaloniki.
- **Tip**: The best spots for water sports in Halkidiki are found along the **Kassandra** coast, especially around **Sani Beach** and **Kallithea**.

3. Hiking Trails: Discover Nature on Foot

Mount Hortiatis

- **What to Expect**: Just a 30-minute drive from Thessaloniki, Mount Hortiatis offers scenic hiking trails through dense forests and breathtaking views of the city and Thermaic Gulf.
- **Difficulty**: Trails range from moderate to challenging, with some steep climbs.
- **Facilities**: There are no major facilities, so bring water, snacks, and wear sturdy hiking boots. The trails are well-marked, but a map or GPS is advisable.
- **How to Get There**: Accessible by car or taxi from the city center.
- **Tip**: Go early in the morning during the summer months to avoid the heat and carry plenty of water.

Seih Sou Forest

- **What to Expect**: This large urban forest is perfect for a quick escape into nature. Located just outside Thessaloniki, it offers several trails that are ideal for walking, running, or mountain biking.
- **Difficulty**: Easy to moderate, ideal for casual hikers or those looking for a scenic jog.
- **Facilities:** There are several picnic areas and viewpoints, but there are few food or drink options, so bring your own.
- **How to Get There**: Easily accessible by bus or car from Thessaloniki.

- **Tip**: Ideal for an afternoon walk or bike ride, especially if you're looking to stay close to the city.

4. Parks and Natural Reserves: Escape into Nature

Botanical Gardens of Thessaloniki

- **What to Expect**: Located in Stavroupoli, this serene garden showcases both local and exotic plants. It's a peaceful spot for a walk or to learn about the region's flora.
- **Facilities**: walking paths, shaded areas, and a small café. Informative signs about the plants are scattered throughout the garden.
- **Entry costs approximately €3-€5.**
- **How to Get There**: A short bus or taxi ride from the city center.
- **Tip**: Perfect for a quiet morning or afternoon stroll, away from the city's hustle.

Pasha's Gardens

- **What to Expect**: A lesser-known green space in Thessaloniki, **Pasha's Gardens** offers a peaceful escape with unique, ancient ruins and a mysterious, tranquil atmosphere.

- **Facilities**: There are no formal facilities, but it's a wonderful place for a peaceful walk and exploration.
- **How to Get There**: Located in Ano Poli, easily accessible on foot or by bus from the city center.
- **Tip**: Ideal for history lovers and those seeking a serene, off-the-beaten-path spot.

5. Off-Road Adventures: Thrill Seekers' Delight

Vardar Gorge

- **What to Expect**: About an hour from Thessaloniki, the **Vardar Gorge** offers exciting off-road trails perfect for 4x4 enthusiasts and hikers. The terrain is rugged, and the natural beauty is stunning, with unique geological formations and scenic views.
- **Activities**: off-roading, hiking, and exploring the gorge.
- **How to Get There**: Best reached by 4x4 or guided off-road tours.
- **Tip**: If you're driving yourself, make sure your vehicle is equipped for off-road conditions, and consider joining a guided tour for a safer and more informative experience.

6. ATV and 4x4 Tours: Adventure Awaits

Thessaloniki off-road tours

- **What to Expect**: Join a guided tour to explore the rugged landscapes around Thessaloniki. You'll navigate through forests, hills, and dirt paths in an ATV or 4x4 vehicle.
- **Prices**: Expect to pay between €80 and €150 per person for a half-day tour, which includes equipment, guides, and refreshments.
- **How to Get There**: Most tours offer pick-up services from central Thessaloniki.
- **Tip**: Check tour reviews and book in advance, especially during the summer, as spots can fill up quickly.

7. Cycling Routes: Pedal Through Scenic Views

Nea Paralia Cycling Path

- **What to Expect**: A dedicated cycling path along Thessaloniki's New Waterfront, perfect for a relaxing ride while taking in views of the Aegean Sea. The route is flat, making it accessible for all fitness levels.
- **Facilities**: Several bike rental stations are available, and there are plenty of cafes and refreshment stands along the way.
- **Prices**: Bike rentals range from €10-€20 per hour.
- **How to get there:** The city center is easily accessible. Bike rental stations are scattered along the waterfront.

- **Tip:** The early morning is the best time for a ride because the waterfront is quieter, and you can enjoy a stunning sunrise over the sea.

8. Villages Around Thessaloniki: Charming Day Trips

Epanomi

- **What to Expect**: A picturesque village known for its vineyards and traditional Greek architecture. It's famous for its wines, particularly **Malagousia**, and offers peaceful strolls through charming streets.
- **Activities**: wine tasting, exploring local shops, and enjoying authentic Greek meals at local tavernas.
- **How to Get There**: About a 30-minute drive from Thessaloniki.
- **Tip:** For a wine tasting experience, try visiting one of the local wineries, such as Ktima Gerovassiliou, which is known for its excellent wines.

Ano Poli (Old Town Thessaloniki)

- **What to Expect**: A historic neighborhood with narrow cobblestone streets, traditional houses, and panoramic views of the city. The area is rich in history, with several Byzantine walls and monuments to explore.

- **Activities**: walking tours, dining in traditional tavernas, and visiting the **Trigonion Tower** for incredible city views.
- **How to Get There**: Easily accessible by bus or a short taxi ride from the city center.
- **Tip**: Spend some time in a local café and try **bougatsa**, a traditional pastry, for a true Thessaloniki experience.

9. Day Trips and Excursions: Explore Beyond Thessaloniki

Mount Olympus

- **What to Expect**: Greece's highest mountain, rich with mythology and natural beauty. The mountain offers incredible hiking trails that range from straightforward walks to challenging treks to the summit.
- **Activities**: hiking, exploring ancient ruins, and enjoying scenic views.
- **How to Get There**: Around 1.5 hours by car from Thessaloniki.
- **Tip**: For a more relaxed experience, hike to **Prionia** and enjoy the lower trails, or explore the **Dion Archaeological Park** at the foot of the mountain.

Halkidiki Peninsula

- **What to Expect**: Known for its beautiful beaches, crystal-clear waters, and charming seaside towns. Halkidiki is divided into three "legs" (Kassandra, Sithonia, and Mount Athos), each offering unique experiences.
- **Activities**: swimming, sunbathing, hiking, and exploring traditional Greek villages.
- **How to Get There**: Around a 1-hour drive from Thessaloniki.
- **Tip**: Visit the quieter **Sithonia** leg if you want fewer crowds and more secluded beaches.

Bonus Outdoor Adventures

Litochoro

- **What to Expect**: A quaint village at the foot of Mount Olympus, **Litochoro** offers excellent opportunities for hiking, exploring traditional Greek culture, and enjoying local cuisine.
- **Activities**: hiking to the **Enipeas Gorge**, exploring local markets, and relaxing at traditional cafes.
- **How to Get There**: A 1.5-hour drive from Thessaloniki.
- **Tip**: Hike the **Enipeas Gorge** for a scenic adventure through waterfalls and lush forests.

Petralona Cave

- **What to Expect**: Located about an hour's drive from Thessaloniki, **Petralona Cave** is famous for its prehistoric findings, including the remains of a 700,000-year-old skull.
- **Activities**: guided cave tours, learning about prehistoric artifacts, and exploring the nearby **Anthropological Museum**.
- **How to Get There**: A 1-hour drive from Thessaloniki.
- **Tip**: Perfect for history and geology enthusiasts looking for a unique adventure.

CHAPTER EIGHT

Shopping in Thessaloniki: An Overview

Thessaloniki is a city where shopping feels like an adventure. Whether you're strolling down lively streets lined with boutiques, hunting for unique souvenirs in bustling markets, or savoring local flavors, Thessaloniki's shopping scene offers something for everyone.

This guide will help you explore the best shopping spots, uncover unique local markets, and find the perfect keepsakes to remember your visit.

Main Shopping Streets

1. Tsimiski Street

- **Overview**: Overview: Tsimiski Street is the heart of Thessaloniki's shopping district, stretching from the historic center to the sea. It's a bustling thoroughfare filled with a wide variety of stores.
- **What to Find**: high-street brands such as Zara, H&M, and Mango, as well as specialty shops. You'll also find electronics stores, beauty products, department stores, cosmetics, and electronics and more
- **Vibe**: Fast-paced and bustling, perfect for those who want a variety of stores in one place.
- **How to Get There**: Located in the heart of the city, easily walkable from most central hotels and accessible via public transport.

2. Mitropolos Street

- **Overview**: Mitropoleos is home to many upscale shops and luxury boutiques, offering a more refined shopping experience compared to Tsimiski.

- **What to Find**: Designer clothing, fine jewelry, luxury watches, and leather goods.
- **Vibe**: Elegant and upscale.
- **How to Get There**: It runs parallel to Tsimiski Street, making it easily accessible from the main shopping area.

3. Agias Sofias Street

- **Overview**: This street offers a mix of modern and traditional Greek shopping, with a focus on local boutiques and artisan shops.
- **What to Find**: Unique fashion pieces, handmade jewelry, and local crafts.
- **Vibe**: quieter and more relaxed compared to Tsimiski and Mitropoleos.
- **How to Get There**: Centrally located, a short walk from the main shopping district.

4. Venizelou Street

- **Overview**: Venizelou Street offers a variety of specialty shops and is great for more eclectic, off-the-beaten-path shopping.
- **What to Find**: Books, music, and unique fashion pieces.
- **Vibe**: varied and eclectic, with a more laid-back atmosphere.

- **How to Get There**: Located near the city center, easily reachable by foot or a short taxi ride.

Boutique Shops

1. Bessies Boutique

- **What to Expect**: This boutique offers elegant clothing and accessories from both local and international designers.
- **Location**: Agias Sofias Street.
- **Price Range**: Mid to high-end, with prices ranging from €50 to €300.

2. Anastasia's Vintage Shop

- **What to Expect**: Anastasia's is a popular spot for vintage lovers, offering clothing and accessories from various decades.
- **Location**: Tsimiski Street.
- **Price range:** affordable to mid-range, from €20 to €100.

3. The Greek Collection

- **What to expect**: This boutique specializes in Greek-designed fashion and artisanal products.
- **Location**: Mitropolos Street.

- **Price range**: mid-range, with items typically costing between €30 and €150.

4. Lefteris Leatherworks

- **What to expect**: Lefteris Leatherworks focuses on handmade, high-quality leather goods.
- **Location**: Venizelou Street.
- **Price Range**: Mid to high-end, with prices ranging from €50 to €200.

5. Artisanal creations

- **What to expect**: This store offers handmade pottery, jewelry, and home décor items.
- **Location**: Agias Sofias Street.
- **Price Range**: mid-range, with prices typically between €30 and €120.

Duty-Free Shopping

Thessaloniki Airport (Makedonia Airport)

- **Overview**: The duty-free shops at Thessaloniki Airport offer a wide range of products, including perfumes, cosmetics, alcohol, tobacco, and local products such as olive oil and sweets.

- **Prices**: Duty-free prices are generally 10-20% lower than retail, though savings can vary depending on the item.
- **How to Get There:** The airport's departure area is accessible after security.
- **Tip**: Correct. You'll need your passport for duty-free purchases, especially for alcohol and tobacco.

Souvenirs and crafts: Take home a piece of Greece

Popular Souvenirs

1. **Greek Olive Oil**:

    o **What to expect**: Thessaloniki offers high-quality olive oil from local producers, renowned for its rich flavor.
    o Modiano Market, Kapani Market, and specialty stores are all places to buy.
    o Price Range: €10 to €30 per bottle.
2. **Mastiha Products**:

    o **What to expect**: Mastiha from the island of Chios is popular in Greece and is used in various products.
    o **Where to Buy**: specialty stores and markets.

- Price Range: €5 to €20.
3. **Greek Honey**:

   - **What to expect**: Greek honey, especially thyme honey, is highly prized.
   - **Markets and local shops are where to buy.**
   - **Price Range**: €10 to €25 per jar.
4. **Traditional Greek sweets**:

   - **What to expect**: Baklava, loukoumi (Turkish delight), and kourabiedes are some of the most popular sweets.
   - **Where to buy**: Confectionery shops and markets.
   - **Price Range**: €5 to €15 per box.
5. **Greek Wine**:

   - **What to expect**: Greek wines, such as Assyrtiko and Xinomavro, are highly regarded.
   - **Where to Buy**: Wine shops, markets, and specialty stores.
   - **Price Range**: €10 to €50 per bottle.

Traditional Crafts

1. **Handwoven Textiles**:

- What to expect: Thessaloniki offers a variety of traditional textiles, including scarves and tablecloths.
- Where to Buy: Artisan shops and markets.
- Price Range: €30 to €100.

2. **Pottery**:

   - What to expect: Handmade pottery with Greek designs is a popular souvenir.
   - Where to buy: artisans shops and local markets.
   - Price Range: €20 to €80.

3. **Handmade Jewelry**:

   - What to expect: Greek artisans craft unique jewelry pieces often inspired by ancient designs.
   - Where to Buy: Boutique shops and artisan markets.
   - Price Range: €20 to €150.

4. **Wood Carvings**:

   - What to expect: Intricately carved wooden items are available as home décor or religious icons.
   - Where to Buy: Artisan shops and markets.
   - Price Range: €25 to €75.

5. **Traditional Greek embroidery**:

- ○ **What to expect**: Beautifully embroidered tablecloths and napkins are common souvenirs.
- ○ **Where to Buy**: Artisan shops and markets.
- ○ **Price Range**: €30 to €100.

Thessaloniki's shopping scene offers a delightful mix of local products, artisan crafts, and high-street brands. From lively markets like **Modiano** and **Kapani**, where you can find fresh food and traditional products, to boutique shops on **Tsimiski** and **Agias Sofias Streets**, the city is perfect for finding unique souvenirs and keepsakes. Whether you're looking for high-quality olive oil, handmade jewelry, or traditional Greek sweets, you'll find something special to take home.

CHAPTER NINE

Glossary of Thessaloniki Terms

Understanding local terms and phrases can significantly enhance your travel experience in Thessaloniki. This glossary includes common Greek phrases, useful travel terms, and local cultural references to help you navigate the city with ease and confidence. Whether you're ordering a meal, asking for directions, or engaging in local customs, these terms will be invaluable.

Common Greek phrases

1. Kaliméra (Καλημέρα)

- **Meaning:** Good morning
- **Usage:** Greet people in the morning until around noon. It's a friendly way to start a conversation or say hello.

2. Kalispera (Καλησπέρα)

- **Meaning:** Good evening
- **Usage:** Use this greeting from around 4 PM until nightfall. It's a polite way to say hello as the day winds down.

3. Kalinihta (Καληνύχτα)

- **Meaning:** Good night

- **Usage:** Use this when saying goodbye in the evening or before going to bed.

4. Efcharistó (Ευχαριστώ)

- **Meaning:** Thank you
- **Usage:** A crucial phrase for expressing gratitude in various situations, from dining to receiving assistance.

5. Parakaló (Παρακαλώ)

- **Meaning:** Please/You're welcome
- **Usage:** Use this term when making a request or when someone thanks you. It's also used as a polite way to say "you're welcome."

6. Sígnomi (Συγγνώμη)

- **Meaning:** Excuse me/I'm sorry
- **Usage:** Use this phrase to apologize or to get someone's attention.

7. Pósa kosta (Πόσα κοστίζει)

- **Meaning:** How much does it cost?
- **Usage:** useful when shopping or inquiring about prices.

8. Éna (Ένα)

- **Meaning:** One
- **Usage:** Handy for ordering food or drinks or when counting.

9. Dýo (Δύο)

- **Meaning:** Two
- **Usage:** useful for ordering multiple items or specifying quantities.

10. Pió (Ποιό)

- **Meaning:** Which
- **Usage:** Useful for asking questions like "Which way?" or "Which item?"

11. Posé (Πως)

- **Meaning:** How
- **Usage:** Use this when asking, "How are you?" or "How does this work?"

12. Poú (Που)

- **Meaning:** Where
- **Usage:** Use this term when asking for directions or locations.

13. Tí (Τι)

- **Meaning:** What
- **Usage:** Useful for asking questions like "What is this?" or "What time?"

14. Sás (Σας)

- **Meaning:** You (plural or formal)

- **Usage:** Used in formal situations or when addressing more than one person.

15. Mí (Μη)

- **Meaning:** No
- **Usage:** Use this to indicate negation or refusal.

16. Né (Ναι)

- **Meaning:** Yes
- **Usage:** Use this to agree or confirm something.

17. Kápoio (Κάποιο)

- **Meaning:** Some / A certain
- **Usage:** Handy for indicating an unspecified quantity or specific thing.

18. Sféti (Σφέτη)

- **Meaning:** This (feminine)
- **Usage:** useful for specifying a particular item or object.

19. Skáfi (Σκάφη)

- **Meaning:** Ship / Boat
- **Usage:** Often used in discussions related to travel or waterfront activities.

20. Póti (Πότι)

- **Meaning:** Drink

- **Usage:** Used when asking for a drink or referring to beverages.

Useful Travel Terms

1. Taxi (Ταξί)

- **Meaning:** Taxi
- **Usage:** Easily recognizable, this term is used to request a taxi. Look for yellow taxis with a "TAXI" sign on top.

2. Leofório (Λεωφορείο)

- **Meaning:** Bus
- **Usage:** Use this term when asking about or inquiring about bus routes and schedules.

3. Stathmós (Σταθμός)

- **Meaning:** Station
- **Usage:** Refers to transport stations, like train or bus stations.

4. Kafeneío (Καφενείο)

- **Meaning:** Café
- **Usage:** A traditional term for a local coffee shop or café.

5. Diakopés (Διακοπές)

- **Meaning:** Vacation / Holidays

- **Usage:** When discussing plans or asking about holiday recommendations.

6. Xénodoxheio (Ξενοδοχείο)

- **Meaning:** Hotel
- **Usage:** useful when looking for accommodation or checking into a hotel.

7. Eíseresi (Είσοδος)

- **Meaning:** Entrance
- **Usage:** Signage is often used in buildings or venues to indicate the entrance.

8. Exódo (Έξοδος)

- **Meaning:** Exit
- **Usage:** Signage used to indicate the way out.

9. Áto (Ατό)

- **Meaning:** Person
- **Usage:** Useful for discussing numbers of people or referring to someone.

10. Tapí (Τάπι)

- **Meaning:** Map
- **Usage:** Handy when asking for or using a map.

11. Plíro (Πλήρω)

- **Meaning:** Payment

- **Usage:** useful in discussions about paying bills or making transactions.

12. Apóstele (Απόσπασμα)

- **Meaning:** receipt
- **Usage:** Use this when asking for a receipt or proof of payment.

13. Eínai (Είναι)

- **Meaning:** It is
- **Usage:** Useful in forming sentences and asking questions, e.g., "Is it far?"

14. Kínisi (Κίνηση)

- **Meaning:** Movement/TTraffic
- **Usage:** refers to traffic conditions or movement in general.

15. Metá (Μετά)

- **Meaning:** After/LLater
- **Usage:** Handy for discussing times or planning.

16. Próto (Πρώτο)

- **Meaning:** First
- **Usage:** useful when ordering or giving directions.

17. Deutéro (Δεύτερο)

- **Meaning:** Second
- **Usage:** helpful for ordering or sequencing items.

18. Káto (Κάτω)

- **Meaning:** Down/BBelow
- **Usage:** Use this for directions or to describe location.

19. Pánw (Πάνω)

- **Meaning:** Up / Above
- **Usage:** Use for directions or describing something that's high.

20. Díkaío (Δίκαιο)

- **Meaning:** Fair/RRight
- **Usage:** useful in discussions about justice or correctness.

Local Terms and Cultural References

1. Ouzo (Ούζο)

- **Meaning:** A traditional Greek alcoholic drink flavored with anise.
- **Usage:** Commonly enjoyed as an aperitif, often accompanied by meze (small dishes).

2. Meze (Μεζές)

- **Meaning:** Small dishes or appetizers served with drinks.
- **Usage:** A staple of Greek dining culture, often enjoyed with friends and family.

3. Gyro (Γύρος)

- **Meaning:** A popular Greek fast food made of meat cooked on a vertical rotisserie.

- **Usage:** Common street food, often served in pita bread with vegetables and sauces.

4. Souvlaki (Σουβλάκι)

- **Meaning:** skewered and grilled meat, usually served with pita and vegetables.

- **Usage:** Another popular Greek street food, often enjoyed with tzatziki sauce.

5. Tzatziki (Τζατζίκι)

- **Meaning:** A Greek dip made from yogurt, cucumbers, garlic, and dill.

- **Usage:** Commonly served as a side dish or dip with bread or meat dishes.

6. Kafenio (Καφενείο)

- **Meaning:** Traditional Greek café, often serving coffee and light snacks.

- **Usage:** A cultural staple where locals gather to socialize.

7. Plaka (Πλάκα)

- **Meaning:** A historic neighborhood in Athens, but the term may be used in Thessaloniki to refer to traditional or historic areas.

- **Usage:** Used to describe charming, historic neighborhoods.

8. Retsina (Ρετσίνα)

- **Meaning:** A Greek wine flavored with pine resin.
- **Usage:** Often enjoyed with Greek food, particularly in traditional tavernas.

9. Kefi (Κέφι)

- **Meaning:** Spirit or joy.
- **Usage:** Used to describe the lively, joyful atmosphere often found in Greek social settings.

10. Zorba (Ζορμπάς)

- **Meaning:** Refers to the famous Greek dance and character from the novel and film "Zorba the Greek."
- **Usage:** Often used to describe energetic dancing or spirited personality.

11. Palió (Παλαιό)

- **Meaning:** Old
- **Usage:** Used to describe something that is ancient or traditional.

12. Néa (Νέα)

- **Meaning:** New
- **Usage:** Used for describing new or modern things.

13. Aníkti (Ανοιχτή)

- **Meaning:** Open
- **Usage:** Commonly seen on signs indicating that a store or business is open.

14. Kleistí (Κλειστή)

- **Meaning:** Closed
- **Usage:** Used on signs to indicate that a store or business is closed.

15. Épiskepsi (Επίσκεψη)

- **Meaning:** Visit
- **Usage:** Useful when discussing plans to visit a place or someone.

16. Eukharistía (Ευχαριστία)

- **Meaning:** Gratitude
- **Usage:** Used to express thankfulness in a more formal context.

17. Anamnisi (Ανάμνηση)

- **Meaning:** memory/ souvenir
- **Usage:** useful when talking about memories or souvenirs from your travels.

18. Parántisi (Παράδοση)

- **Meaning:** Tradition
- **Usage:** Used when referring to cultural practices or traditional events.

19. Aforí (Αφορί)

- **Meaning:** Exemption
- **Usage:** Used in contexts related to taxes or rules.

20. Sýn (Σύν)

- **Meaning:** Together
- **Usage:** Used in phrases like "We are together" or when discussing group activities.

Greek phrases for everyday conversations

1. How are you?

- **Greek:** Τι κάνετε; (Ti kánate?) [Formal]
- **Greek:** Τι κάνεις (Ti káneis?) [Informal]
- **Pronunciation:** Tee KAH-nay-teh?/Tee KAH-nees?
- **Usage:** Use this phrase to ask someone how they are doing. "Ti kánate?" is more appropriate in formal settings or when addressing someone with respect, while "Ti káneis?" is used among friends or people you are familiar with.

2. What is your name?

- **Greek:** Πώς σε λένε; (Pós se léne?) [Informal]
- **Greek:** Πώς σας λένε; (Pós sas léne?) [Formal]
- **Pronunciation:** Pohs seh LEH-neh? / Pohs sahs LEH-neh?

- **Usage:** Use "Pós se léne?" when asking someone's name in a casual setting. "Pós sas léne?" is for formal situations or when addressing someone you don't know well.

3. My name is...

- **Greek:** Το όνομά μου είναι... (To ónomá mou íne...)
- **Pronunciation:** To OH-noh-mah moo EE-neh...
- **Usage:** Use this phrase to introduce yourself. Simply follow it with your name.

4. Where are you from?

- **Greek:** Από πού είστε; (Apó poú íste?) [Formal]
- **Greek:** Από πού είσαι; (Apó poú íse?) [Informal]
- **Pronunciation:** Ah-POH poo EE-steh? / Ah-POH poo EE-seh?
- **Usage:** Use "Apó poú íste?" in formal settings or with strangers, and "Apó poú íse?" with friends or peers.

5. Where are you going?

- **Greek:** Πού πηγαίνετε; (Poú piyénate?) [Formal]
- **Greek:** Πού πας; (Poú pas?) [Informal]
- **Pronunciation:** Poo pee-YEH-neh-teh? / Poo pahs?
- **Usage:** Ask "Poo piyénate?" when speaking formally or inquiring about someone's plans in a respectful manner. "Poo pas?" is more casual and suitable for friends.

6. I will see you tomorrow.

- **Greek:** Τα λέμε αύριο. (Ta léme ávrio.)
- **Pronunciation:** Tah LEH-meh AH-vree-oh
- **Usage:** Use this phrase to say goodbye with the intention of meeting again the next day.

7. What food do you have?

- **Greek:** Τι φαγητά έχετε; (Ti fagitá éhete?) [Formal]
- **Greek:** Τι φαγητά έχεις; (Ti fagitá éhis?) [Informal]
- **Pronunciation:** Tee fah-yee-TAH EH-heh-teh? / Tee fah-yee-TAH EH-hees?
- **Usage:** Use "Ti fagitá éhete?" when inquiring about the food options in a formal setting or at a restaurant. "Ti fagitá éhis?" is used in a more casual context.

8. What drinks do you have?

- **Greek:** Τι ποτά έχετε; (Ti potá éhete?) [Formal]
- **Greek:** Τι ποτά έχεις; (Ti potá éhis?) [Informal]
- **Pronunciation:** Tee poh-TAH EH-heh-teh? / Tee poh-TAH EH-hees?
- **Usage:** Use "Ti potá éhete?" to ask about drink options in a more formal setting. "Ti potá éhis?" is for informal contexts.

9. How much is it?

- **Greek:** Πόσο κοστίζει; (Póso kostízei?)

- **Pronunciation:** POH-soh koh-STEH-zee?

- **Usage:** Use this phrase when inquiring about the cost of an item or service.

10. Can you help me?

- **Greek:** Μπορείτε να με βοηθήσετε; (Boreíte na me voithísete?) [Formal]

- **Greek:** Μπορείς να με βοηθήσεις; (Boreís na me voithíseis?) [Informal]

- **Pronunciation:** Boh-REE-teh nah meh voe-THEE-seh-teh? / Boh-REES nah meh voe-THEE-sees?

- **Usage:** Use "Boreíte na me voithísete?" in formal situations or when asking for help from someone you don't know well. "Boreís na me voithíseis?" is more casual.

11. Excuse me, where is...?

- **Greek:** Συγγνώμη, πού είναι...; (Signómi, poú íne...?)

- **Pronunciation:** See-NOH-mee, poo EE-neh...?

- **Usage:** Use this phrase when asking for directions or locating something. Follow it with the place or item you are looking for.

12. I don't understand.

- **Greek:** Δεν καταλαβαίνω. (Den katalavaino.)

- **Pronunciation:** Then ka-ta-la-VEH-noh

- **Usage:** Use this phrase if you're having trouble understanding what someone is saying.

13. Could you speak slower, please?

- **Greek:** Μπορείτε να μιλήσετε πιο αργά, παρακαλώ; (Boreíte na milísete pio argá, parakaló?)

- **Pronunciation:** Boh-REE-teh nah mee-LEE-seh-teh pee-oh ar-GAH, pah-rah-kah-LOH?

- **Usage:** This is helpful if you need someone to slow down their speech so you can understand better.

14. I would like...

- **Greek:** Θα ήθελα... (Tha íthela...)

- **Pronunciation:** Tha EE-theh-lah...

- **Usage:** Use this phrase to politely state what you would like, whether it's a dish at a restaurant or something you want to buy.

15. Can I pay by credit card?

- **Greek:** Μπορώ να πληρώσω με πιστωτική κάρτα; (Boró na pliróso me pistotikí kárta?)

- **Pronunciation:** Bo-ROH nah plee-ROH-soh meh pees-toh-TEE-kee KAR-tah?

- **Usage:** Use this phrase to inquire whether you can use a credit card for payment.

16. Where is the bathroom?

- **Greek:** Πού είναι η τουαλέτα; (Poú íne i toualéta?)

- **Pronunciation:** Poo EE-neh ee too-ah-LEH-tah?
- **Usage:** This phrase will help you locate the bathroom or restroom.

17. I am lost.

- **Greek:** Έχω χαθεί. (Écho chatheí.)
- **Pronunciation:** EH-hoh kha-THEE
- **Usage:** Use this phrase if you find yourself disoriented and need assistance finding your way.

18. Do you speak English?

- **Greek:** Μιλάτε αγγλικά; (Miláte angliká?) [Formal]
- **Greek:** Μιλάς αγγλικά; (Milás angliká?) [Informal]
- **Pronunciation:** Mee-LAH-teh ang-lee-KAH? / Mee-LAHS ang-lee-KAH?
- **Usage:** Use "Miláte angliká?" in formal situations or with strangers, and "Milás angliká?" with friends or peers.

19. What time is it?

- **Greek:** Τι ώρα είναι; (Ti óra íne?)
- **Pronunciation:** Tee OR-ah EE-neh?
- **Usage:** Ask this when you need to know the current time.

20. I'm sorry.

- **Greek:** Συγγνώμη. (Signómi.)

- **Pronunciation:** See-NOH-mee

- **Usage:** Use this phrase to apologize or get someone's attention politely.

21. Can I have the menu, please?

- **Greek:** Μπορώ να δω το μενού, παρακαλώ; (Boró na do to mení, parakaló?)

- **Pronunciation:** Bo-ROH nah tho toh meh-NEE, pah-rah-kah-LOH?

- **Usage:** Use this phrase at a restaurant when you need to see the menu.

22. How do you say this in Greek?

- **Greek:** Πώς λέγεται αυτό στα ελληνικά; (Pós légetai aftó sta elliniká?)

- **Pronunciation:** Pohs LEH-yeh-teh af-TOH stah eh-lee-nee-KAH?

- **Usage:** Use this phrase if you want to know how to say something in Greek.

practice and listen to Greek pronunciation

To practice and listen to Greek pronunciation, there are several useful tools and resources available online. Here are some of the best options:

1. Forvo

- **Description:** Forvo is a pronunciation dictionary where you can listen to native speakers pronounce words and phrases in various languages, including Greek.

- **Website:** Forvo
- **How to Use:** Search for Greek phrases or words, and listen to the audio recordings by native speakers.

2. Google Translate

- **Description:** Google Translate offers pronunciation for many languages. While it may not always be perfect, it's a good tool for hearing how words and phrases are pronounced.
- **Website:** Google Translate
- **How to Use:** Enter Greek words or phrases and click the speaker icon to hear the pronunciation.

3. Merriam-Webster's Greek-English Dictionary

- **Description:** This resource provides pronunciations for Greek words and phrases and often includes phonetic spellings.
- **Website:** Merriam-Webster
- **How to Use:** Search for Greek words or phrases and listen to their pronunciations.

4. Linguee

- **Description:** Linguee provides example sentences and pronunciation for many languages. It's particularly useful for seeing phrases in context.

- **Website:** Linguee
- **How to Use:** Search for Greek phrases and listen to their pronunciation, or read sentences with audio pronunciations.

6. **Duolingo**

- **Description:** Duolingo is a language-learning app that includes pronunciation practice for Greek and other languages.
- **Website:** Duolingo
- **How to Use:** Download the app and practice Greek by listening to and repeating phrases.

7. **Pimsleur**

- **Description:** Pimsleur offers audio-based language learning courses with a focus on pronunciation and conversational skills.
- **Website:** Pimsleur
- **How to Use:** Purchase a Greek course and follow the audio lessons to practice pronunciation and conversation.

8. **Glossika**

- **Description:** Glossika provides language learning through audio sentences, helping with pronunciation and fluency.
- **Website:** Glossika

- **How to Use:** Use their Greek language modules to practice pronunciation through repeated listening and speaking exercises.

9. Speechling

- **Description:** Speechling offers pronunciation practice by comparing your speech to native speakers and receiving feedback.
- **Website:** Speechling
- **How to Use:** Record your pronunciation and compare it with native speakers to improve your accuracy.

10. Rosetta Stone

- **Description:** Rosetta Stone provides comprehensive language learning tools, including pronunciation practice with immediate feedback.
- **Website:** Rosetta Stone
- **How to Use:** Enroll in their Greek language course and practice pronunciation through their interactive platform.

CONCLUSION

Saying Goodbye to Thessaloniki: A Journey to Remember

As your journey through Thessaloniki comes to a close, take a moment to reflect on the vibrant experiences, unforgettable flavors, and breathtaking sights this remarkable city has offered. From the bustling markets and charming streets to the serene beaches and rich historical sites, Thessaloniki has woven its unique charm into every moment of your visit.

Saying Goodbye to Thessaloniki

Leaving Thessaloniki can feel like saying goodbye to an old friend. The city's warm hospitality, rich history, and lively atmosphere have likely left a lasting impression. As you prepare to head home, here's a guide to ensure you leave with cherished memories and a sense of fulfillment:

- **Embrace the Memories**: Reflect on your favorite moments, whether it was witnessing a stunning sunset by the sea, savoring a delicious meal at a local taverna, or exploring a captivating historical site. These memories will stay with you long after you've left.

- **Capture Your Moments**: Take those last few photos of your favorite spots—the iconic White Tower, the vibrant Ladadika District, or the peaceful Vlatadon Monastery. These images will serve as treasured reminders of your Greek adventure.

- **Express Your Gratitude**: If you've had memorable interactions with locals, don't forget to say "efcharistó" (thank you). It's a small but meaningful way to show your appreciation for the city's hospitality.

- **Plan Your Return**: Thessaloniki has a way of calling travelers back. Keep an eye out for upcoming events or festivals you may want to experience on your next visit. The city's dynamic nature ensures there's always something new to discover.

Final Tips for Travelers

Before you set off on your journey home, here are a few tips to ensure a smooth departure and make your future return to Thessaloniki even more enjoyable:

- ❖ **Review Your Checklist**: Double-check your travel documents, souvenirs, and any last-minute items.

Make sure nothing gets left behind.

- ❖ **Local Currency**: If you have leftover euros, consider spending them before you leave, as many places in Thessaloniki prefer cash. Otherwise, exchange them at the airport or hold onto them for future visits.

- ❖ **Transport to the Airport**: Ensure your transportation to the airport is sorted. Public transport in Thessaloniki is reliable, but if you're carrying heavy luggage, a taxi may offer more convenience.

- ❖ **Souvenirs and Gifts**: If you're bringing back local treasures, be mindful of customs regulations, especially when it comes to food, plants, or other restricted items.

- ❖ **Travel Apps and Maps:** For your journey, download any required travel apps or offline maps. This is especially useful if you'll be traveling to areas with limited internet access.

- ❖ **Stay Connected**: If you've made new friends or contacts in Thessaloniki, exchange contact details before you leave. A quick message or email can help maintain those connections.

❖ **Reflect and Relax**: Once the logistics are handled, take a moment to relax. Reflect on your journey, the places you've seen, and the people you've met. A peaceful mind will make your transition home smoother.

❖ **Stay Informed**: Keep an eye on any travel advisories or regulation changes that might affect your return journey. Staying informed will help ensure a hassle-free departure.

❖ **Leave Feedback**: If you've had excellent service at hotels, restaurants, or tours, consider leaving a review. Positive feedback supports local businesses and helps other travelers find excellent experiences.

❖ **Look Forward**: As you leave Thessaloniki, start planning your next adventure—whether it's a return visit to this beautiful city or exploring new destinations. The joy of discovery will always be with you.

Farewell, Thessaloniki, Until Next Time

Thessaloniki's rich history, vibrant culture, and warm people have made your stay truly special. As you depart, carry with you the joy of exploration and the fondness for a city that welcomes travelers with open arms.

Safe travels, until next time!

Printed in Great Britain
by Amazon

60587860R00107